Wham Bam

thank you

GLAM

SHREWSBURY COLLEGE
LONDON RD LRC

First published in Great Britain 1998
by Aurum Press Ltd,
25 Bedford Avenue
London WC1B 3AT

Copyright © 1998 JMP Ltd

Jeremy Novick and Mick Middles have
asserted their moral right to be identified as
the authors of this work in accordance with the
Copyright, Designs and Patents Act 1987

A catalogue record for this book is available
from the British Library

ISBN 1 85410 587 6

Design by Will Harvey for JMP Ltd
Picture research by Karen Tucker for JMP Ltd

Printed and bound in Great Britain by
Jarrold Book Printing, Thetford.

Introduction

Where Do I Begin?

What was the Seventies? A decade that had Nicolas Roeg and Donald Cammell's psychotropic *Performance*, with its gender confusions and personality crises breaking down the walls of society at one end, and Francis Coppola's *Apocalypse Now* at the other end. What happened in between? That was some journey.

In 1972, Slade traded blows with Alice Cooper while in the other semi-final Lieutenant Pigeon played The Royal Scots Dragoon Guards Band. But music was always mad in the Seventies. In 1973, when Glam was at its height and even Mrs Greenberg who worked in the local baker had dyed hair (OK so it was a blue rinse – don't get bogged down in detail) what was the top single? Eye Level by the Simon Park Orchestra. Yes, yes, the theme to *Van Der Valk*. An if you can't remember it, just be grateful you're not reading this in ten years. Odds on, then we'll have 'artificially intelligent' books which will play you snatches of each song mentioned in the text.

Albums-wise, the best-selling nonsense were those compilations of old Sixties hits that were put out by companies like K-Tel and Ronco, companies who made labour saving devices called like the Buttonmatic, which was an automatic button-sewing machine, presumably for buttons which didn't want to try too hard.

While we're talking about objects that are remembered through their adverts, do you remember the adverts for Mannekin cigars? Rampant naked women swinging through the jungle. Or St. Bruno. I think that was the best one. A Milk Tray man is followed by hundreds of gorgeous chicks and then he instructs his bald minder to let one of them through. Then the pay off-line... the sales pitch at the end informed us that St Bruno was 'ready-rubbed'.

Was that a gag?

Tubular Bells, Mike Oldfield's opus, was huge. Richard Branson's first release on his new Virgin record label, it brought in enough revenue to pave the way for all Virgin's future successes. I wonder. I wonder what would have happened if Joe Public had thought 'Tubular Balls, more like'.

It's difficult to know what was the catalyst, the moment when everything went Glam. It's difficult, and listen, I hate to get all bookish about this, but if you want to know about today, you've got to look at yesterday, you know what I mean? Maybe it's time for a bit of history, a bit of context.

In a book not too dissimilar to this one, it is written 'and the meek shall inherit the earth'. Well, that might have been true once, but that was then and this is now and right here in the West no one is too interested in all that hanging around. We won the war and to the victor the spoils. No one wants to spend their life waiting for the will to be read. Inheritances, inschmeritances. Get yourself a couple of sharp lawyers, get me Whiplash Willie and contest the thing. The meek? Whaddya mean the goddamn meek? Get outta here! I lived here all my goddamn life!

That, basically, is the story of how Glam came about. It's the story of every youth movement thrown up after the war since the teenager was invented in the Fifties. What had started in the Fifties with the Beats and continued into the Sixties with the psychedelic Pranksters and the hippies (American version) and the beat combo and the hippies (English version) had reached a bit of a watershed.

Over there, the Vietnam war had killed off all those naïve ideas about youth culture changing anything as surely as if the napalm had been dropped on them. The psychedelics had long been outlawed – Ken Kesey was in jail, Neal Cassady was dead – and the Woodstock generation had gone their own ways, pausing only to cash the cheque. All that was left were a few earnest cowboys knee deep in denim singing jumped-up country music.

Above: The Rolling Stones' Mick Jagger (he's the one on the right), with Anita Pallenberg, pouting their way through *Performance*.
Opposite: Glam Life at its finest – the megawatt speakers are

Back home, everything had ended, as it had started, with The Beatles. The Beatles split up and, as they did, so too did the rest of youth culture. John sat in bed. Paul did a spot of farming. George went off and saved Bangladesh, and Ringo, bless, sat on the platform and waited for *Thomas The Tank Engine* to pull in.

As the Sixties turned into the Seventies, pop culture had come to recognise that meek was all very well if you just wanted peace, love and understanding, but if you wanted something a bit more? If you wanted more than some grass that made you smile like an idiot and say words like 'man' and 'cool'? If you wanted something a little more – how you say? – tangible than a small piece of card with a pretty picture on it which you swallowed that sent you up there, high to the sky with Lucy and her diamonds? Yeah, well, forget all that sitting cross-legged with an acoustic guitar, a bongo and a bong.

Take Marc Bolan. How Marc Bolan was loved. Everyone loved Marc Bolan – well, everyone apart from my mum. (We grew up in Stamford Hill, the same mid-urban neighbourhood that fed the young Bolan and his boy, David Jones. They used to hang out in the local bowling alley and my mum, a kindly soul who knows one end of a chicken from the other, gave strict instructions that the bowling alley was to be avoided. Odd types hung around there, she reckoned. Me? In my green and black crushed-velvet loon pants, I didn't buy it.)

Anyway, Bolan. Everyone loved Marc Bolan. Throw a free festival and he was there. He'd turn up at the opening of a packet of Rizlas. Loved. Him and his sidekick. He made a record called something like *My People Were Fair And Had Sky In Their Hair But Now They're Content To Wear Stars On Their Brows*. Nice tunes, sweet lyrics. Sensitive. It was a great success, bought by about maybe 30 people. (No doubt they passed it around, but that's not the point.)

But Bolan had been brought up in Stamford Hill and had been chosen to know the value of things. Enough was enough. Cult love fed the chakras but left the tummy empty. Something else was needed. Bolan watched and learned. Out went the dippy hippy and in came the *Electric Warrior*. Loud hair, loud clothes, loud looks. More to the point, loud sales and serious cash. Meek schmeek.

That was it. That was the moment. It was the moment when June Bolan called over to Marc and said, 'Oooh. I wonder what this looks like?' and smeared a load of glitter make-up underneath his eyes.

But how did that spread like a dose of shingles over everything it touched? Look, there have been plenty of funny/glitzy/rubbishy show-offs wearing some funny/glitzy/rubbishy outfit who've burst upon the pop scene, who've made a bit of an impact but who've stayed essentially in the pop universe. Somehow Glam transcended that, it moved from pop into telly and from telly into everything. Obviously things like clothes and fashions were affected – that goes with the pop territory. But cars? Sweets? Adverts? How on earth was Bolan mincing around to Ride A White Swan on *Top Of The Pops* connected to Regan and Carter screeching round the corner in a Ford Granada giving it a load of mouth? The short answer is by a pair of furry dice and it's probably true. Bolan and Regan were connected only in the sense that one begat the other. If Bolan hadn't have got it on or even banged a gong, Regan would have been a very different beast. (Well, he might not have been, but his car would have looked different and his shirt lapels wouldn't have looked quite so much like an African Elephant's ears.)

Marc Bolan had the hair, the stare, the flares and the wide lapels. But he was yet to discover the merits of eye glitter...

You know what they say about comedy, that to analyse it is to kill it. Well, the same is true of this Glam schtick. Me, I think that the best thing is to forget all that sociological stuff. We've spent long enough wondering what is and what isn't. I've got a Fidelity Unit 4 record player that my old man bought me from Woolworth's here, all white with separate speakers and it's great. It plays six records, one after each other, in a row. What do you reckon? OK – Virginia Plain, Get It On, Rock 'n' Roll Pt 1 & 2, Blockbuster, Ride A White Swan, and, of course, Can The Can.

I should co-co.

Jeremy Novick. April 1998.

You Don't Get Me,

Coming directly after the 'white heat' of the Sixties, a time of believable dreams and unbelievable disappointments, the early Seventies was the bill – service not included. Unemployment, three-day weeks, strikes in place of strife, Leyland, Michael Edwardes, Red Robbo, oil grief, Thatcher the Milk-Snatcher (June 1971 – you were warned), Ireland, poverty. Even the Apollo programme blew up in our faces. If we'd have known then about pollution, whales and the ozone what we know now, life would have been complete.

Ever since the Paris student riots of 1968, and London's mini-riot of its own in Grosvenor Square (which led to anti-tank steps being built in front of the American Embassy), the people had been revolting – and I don't just mean in terms of dress. Wimmin (no 'men' in wimmin) had started burning their bras and demanding equality – the silly moos. The dustbin men went on strike for months, although people in South London couldn't tell, and Ted Heath was too busy playing with his organ to notice the winter of discontent blowing around him until he was voted out of office in 1973. Ted was replaced by Harold (again), and to be honest it was difficult to see the difference. The streets which weren't impassable due to the horse-size rats feeding on the bin-bags lying around, were haunted by skinhead gangs out to stomp anybody who wasn't white, working class or bigger than them. The trains were forever being trashed by Inter-city firms of football hooligans with

Skinheads politely queue to give someone a good kicking

lovely names (Mad Dog, Slasher, Shit-for-Brains). Telly (all three channels of it!) went off the air at 11pm. Pounds, shilling and pence was being phased out in favour of, er, pounds and pence.

As politics got greyer and life became more depressing, people needed a break – literally. They needed larger than life figures to take them away from it all. Which is where the Bolans and the Bowies came into it. What joy was there in watching a dirty, gratefully dead hippie who was happy to play long, endlessly long, meandering instrumentals

Eat this! Matters of European Unity roused passions never seen before. Or since

I'm Part Of The Union

because it meant that he didn't have to get up from his stoned stupor?

For Marc Bolan, glitter was a definite decision, a uniform, a look that defined him. Some eyeliner, a bit of something to make him stand out, something that made him sparkle. Like glitter. It worked a treat. Bolan hit upon something that inspired an army of clones who revelled in his success. He shone a light in the hearts of kids who were being brought up in a grey world. It was escapism and realism combined. Hey you! Don't watch that, watch this! You don't have to believe the tales those grown-ups are telling you. *Metal Guru* was no accidental title.

There's nothing radical in this. It's one of the only virtues of the British character, this ability to conjure up the joy to flaunt in the face of the grey. As the last Socialist dream was fading in the glint of Jim Callaghan's spectacles in 1976, Johnny Rotten and Joe Strummer were spitting in the eye of a storm, one which would be whipped up into a full-scale social revolution by a swear word on tea-time television. In the Eighties, when Thatcher was busy selling England by the pound and caring more about some sheep in the southern Atlantic than 'her' people, the youthful reaction was Blitz, Boy George and Marilyn.

The politics of Glam were simple: have a good time, all of the time. Which is why there never was a Glam member of parliament. People were too busy having sex, getting drunk and/or stoned or posing in front of their bedroom mirrors to think about voting for a change. Which is a shame, because if Glam had made its way onto the political stage, who knows what might have happened. We could, even now, be labouring under a government ruled by a small, cheeky chappie with corkscrew hair who drives a Rolls Royce because it's good for his voice. It might have been had Marc only believed that you *can* fool the children of the revolution. ☆☆

A consumer boom resulted in a tide of empty cardboard boxes. Oh, that and the dustmen going on strike

John,

I'm only dancing

'Bolan started the whole Glam thing. He put glitter on his eyelids, then added a pencil line and mascara. He'd wear a velvet jacket with an ostrich feather boa flung around his neck. Glam rock was all about putting on a spectacle. The Glam audience became part of the show. They dressed up and it was like a party.'

Mike Leander, 'the man behind' Gary Glitter

The music of the Glamsters was very definitely music of the now. It was perfect for its time. Think of it as a kind of cultural Darwinism. The survival of the fittest. The evolution of what's right for that time.

But what exactly was Glam music, what exactly was Glam rock?

OK, let me throw this one at you. Which was more Glam? Mud appearing on *Top Of The Pops* or Rick Wakeman doing *The Court Of King Arthur* on ice at Wembley? Let's look at the candidates.

Mud, a bunch-of-lads-on-the-make type of band who were strictly of the 'right time, right place' variety, used to appear in stretchy Dralon trousers and did the cheesiest dance imaginable to the worst song this side of Lieutenant Pigeon.

'That's right, that right, that's right, that's right,
Really love your tiger light.
That's neat, that's neat, that's neat, that's neat,
Really love your tiger feet.'

(Cue two-note Woolworth's guitar solo.)

It's the sort of song that they could have written while awaiting the result of the steward's enquiry on the 3.20 at Haydock Park.

That was Mud.

Rick Wakeman was a different bag of boiled sweets. Wakeman,

you may recall, specialised in these huge, overblown spectacles – no, no, different spectacles. That was Elton John. Pay attention, please – these huge happenings based around historical and literary events. *The Six Wives Of Henry VIII. The Journey To The Centre Of The Earth* and, the daddy of them all, *The Court Of King Arthur…* on ice! It's difficult to convey exactly what it was that Wakeman did, but let's try. He assembled a huge cast of supporting actors – musicians, dancers, horses – while he himself stood at a bank of about 50 keyboards – surrounded by the things, he was – and he'd be there in a flowing glittery full-length cape with long blonde shampoo-ad hair and he would swan around and orchestrate this mad scene with his hair and his cape and the horses on ice-skates. It was mad, and it was the loudest, most ostentatious, most gloriously outrageous pile of twaddle you've ever seen. It probably cost millions – it bankrupted Wakeman – and if there was ever a scene that showed a decadent society sticking two fingers up to the economic hardships of the time, this was it.

So there you go. You've met our contestants in tonight's game of *What's More Glam?*, now using the information that you've been given in this book so far, you must decide who's the glammiest, Mud or Rick Wakeman.

Sorry, I'm going to have to hurry you…

Oh, I'm so sorry. You've chosen the wrong answer. The correct answer was, in fact, Mud.

Why the down-home appeal of Mud and not the overblown glitz of Wakeman? OK, first, I've got to admit it. There was something that I left out of Mud's *Top Of The Pops* description. I left out the bouffant hair, the dress and the earrings that guitarist Rob Davies happened to be wearing. A minor omission, you'll agree. Why Mud? Well, only partly because of the bouffant hair, the dress and the earrings. Mainly it was because of the *Top Of The Pops* connection.

Mud were accessible in a way that Wakeman – a ridiculous example, by the way – wasn't. Glam was, first and foremost, by the kids for the kids. It sounds twee and romantic, but it's actually true. You could play at Glam. You could be any age – as long as it was young. You didn't have to be rich. You didn't have to be (particularly) talented. And you didn't have to be (particularly) good-looking. It was one of those classic DIY movements, something you could do at home. And lastly – but most importantly – it was fun, and fun in

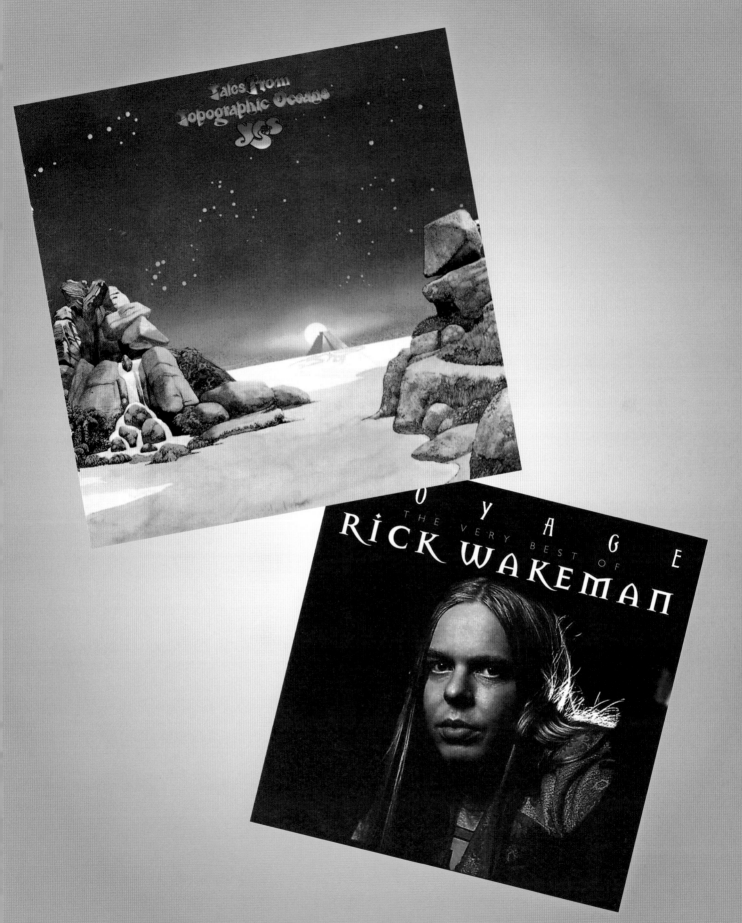

the way the best things in life are: cheap, spontaneous, open. It was people having a laugh – people having a laugh at the world and people having a laugh at themselves. That's why not only was Rick Wakeman not Glam-mer than Mud, he wasn't even in the same ball park. It's also why there's a Glam revival every couple of years.

Listen, if the answer to our question had been Rick Wakeman, this book wouldn't be here.

If you want to get all serious about it, you could say that it was a class difference. One was middle class – it was all 'let's be impressed with the technique. My, you must have worked really hard at school to be able to do that'. The other was working class – 'We'll have a drink now and learn how to play the guitar later.' If you want further proof, in 1973 Wakeman's proper band, Yes, put out a double concept album cailed *Tales From Topographic Oceans* that concerned itself with 'the revealing science of God'. Mud didn't.

Glam laughed in the face of all that pompous pseudo-intellectualism, it declared war on seriousness. You want three day weeks? We want Can The Can. You want *Topographic Oceans*? We want Tiger Feet. That's neat.

It is, of course, the sweetest of all ironies that the first Glam rocker, the man who it could be argued invented the genre, took himself more seriously than a hundred *Topographic Oceans*. He probably thought he *was* a Topographic Ocean.

Glam was the precursor of disco, of punk, of new romantics, of the techno-hippies of the early Nineties. Mostly, it was like the thing which would eventually replace it, punk. Originally there was the Pistols, The Clash and The Damned, remember? And originally everyone got all het up about the Pistols, got all idolatrous about the Clash. And The Damned? Everybody just took the piss out of The Damned. They're like cartoons! They're not real! They don't mean it! Out of the three, easily the most influential were… The Damned. It was their spirit that lived on simply because they were the ones having a laugh., they were your mates. Everyone likes icons such as the Pistols and The Clash, but you look at icons, you gawp in reverence at icons. They're cold and impressive and distant. Mates you have a laugh with.

Glam picked up on the hippie ideal of showing off and took it to a new level. The hippies blew it when they started to take themselves seriously – always the death-knell of any movement – and that was a trap that the Glamsters couldn't fall into. After all, how could you take yourself seriously when you were wearing metallic blue and silver platform boots with a five-inch heel?

Actually, some of them did – most of them did – and as soon as they did, they were finished. Apart from the grand-daddy of the scene we mentioned just before – yes, we're talking about Marc Bolan – most of the Glamsters played with the idea of being sensible, looked at it and laughed at it. Do it while you can.

That Bolan created the scene and then reneged on its dearest condition is funny but obvious. You should know by now that God likes His little gags. The truth is that, again like punk, most of the people involved in Glam probably weren't creative enough to have actually come up with it. It needed someone with that bit of something special, that someone who wanted to stand out of the crowd. Once he'd done that, then everyone could follow. Movements are lovely like that, aren't they? Another of God's little gags. Out of the desire to stand out from the crowd comes... a new crowd.

Metal Guru,

June Bolan called over to Marc and said 'Oooh. I wonder what this looks like?' and smeared a load of glitter make-up underneath his eyes. Was it really that straightforward? David Enthoven was Marc Bolan's manager at the time. 'Yes, it was. Basically Bolan wasn't influenced by anybody. His wife thought it would be quite a neat idea to put some glitter under his eyes. She was a stylist and it was just a good idea.' What else could it have been? Here's this cross-legged pixie folkie and suddenly he's wearing his wife's make-up. Listen, this is a man who got his name by taking the Bo and the Lan from Bob Dylan. 'I thought it was a terrific idea,' shrugs Enthoven. 'When I first saw him, he wasn't really playing much guitar, and I said to him "Why don't you do something with more guitar in it?" and that's when he came up with Ride A White Swan.' So that was after June had put the glitter under his eyes? 'No, it was just at the same time.'

And how did that go down?

'We got into terrible trouble with all his fans, when we started calling it T.Rex and getting him to stand up. But the thing with Marc is that he wanted to be a star, he didn't want to be small and credible.' From the outside it looks like Enthoven and Bolan – and Bolan's wife – sat down with a pen and paper and worked it all out. 'It wasn't as calculated as that,' Enthoven insists. 'All the best ideas come from people just having a bit of fun. There wasn't any great masterplan where we all sat down and said, "Let's re-invent this guy." You know, I'd love to take credit for all that, but it's not true. It was huge fun coming up with the ideas and then seeing it all work. But it was all about having a bit of fun, really, and Bolan took himself very seriously but he was also a very cheeky chappy. He was ambitious. It wouldn't have happened if he hadn't have really wanted it. He liked to go on stage and throw his guitar in the air and do all that. He was a showman.'

Why was the name shortened?

'Because I couldn't spell tyrannosaurus.'

Get out of here.

is it you?

'No really. I couldn't spell tyrannosaurus, and one day I wrote T. Rex down on a bit of paper and Marc saw that and he said "Oh, that looks good. Let's call it T.Rex." When you're on a roll you find that good things start happening because you're doing it right. A lot of times when things start going right, a lot of people get really anal and try and work out why it is that things are going well. That's when things start to go wrong.

Good job Marc's missus' gear fitted him.

'But I have to tell you, there was no grand plan. When you capture the moment, just go with it and if it's the right moment, it will gather its own momentum. If it captures people's imagination and that's what they want, well, go with it.' Did the new Marc hit big immediately? 'Absolutely straight away. As soon as we saw Marc on television we knew. As soon as the camera got hold of him it was obvious. He was very telegenic, but he was asexual, too. He looked like a girl but he was a boy. It was perfect – it captured the moment and it was just what the kids wanted. It was completely different to all the studious hippies that were around at the time. It was sexy.'

He looked like a girl but he was a boy. It was perfect – it captured the moment and it was just what the kids wanted.

T.Rextasy it was called and by 1972 Marc Bolan was the most famous man in England. That Bolan broke big was no surprise. He'd been after it since his early teens. When he was 14, he was featured in *Town*, an early style magazine, as one of the Mod faces about town. Bolan always had an idea of what he wanted and a starving hunger to achieve it. Who, what, where, when and how – that detail would be filled in later. Much later, like when being interviewed, he'd tell people of his time in Paris when he was taken under the wing of a mysterious shamanic character called only The Wizard, who 'educated' him in the black arts. Well, be fair. What was he going to say? "I'm a short Jewish lad on the make"?

When Bolan saw at the end of the 1960s that the hippy-dippy thing was dying on its legs, he, along with all the other Glamstars, looked back to his youth, back to what inspired him, back to a time when you can do what you want, but stay offa my blue suede shoes.

T.Rextasy lasted just over two years and in that time Bolan was king. The hits were classics – **Ride A White Swan** (October 1970), **Hot Love** (April 1971), **Get It On** (July 1971), **Jeepster** (November 1971), **Telegram Sam** (January 1972), **Metal Guru** (May 1972), **Children Of The Revolution** (September 1972) and **Solid Gold Easy Action** (December 1972). But that was it. By the time of **20th Century Boy** (March 1973), the game was up.

Marc Bolan changed the face of pop music – of pop culture – but it ate him. He did what he did and he didn't move on. For contemporaries like The Sweet that was enough, but for Bolan it wasn't – and it ate him. Rejected by the hippies he'd left behind, he found that the ephemeral nature of pop stardom was perhaps a little too ephemeral. What else do you want to know? Cocaine, naturally, did for the rest. A natural punk, Bolan was in mid-rehabilitation when the gods stepped in, and on September 16, 1977 he died, care of a disagreement between his Mini and a sycamore tree in Barnes. He was 29. Death schmeath. Life played the ultimate trick on Marc Bolan long after he had died. What can you do to someone after they're dead, you may think. Well… In 1991, Levi's decided to use 20th Century Boy to advertise their jeans. Can you imagine? Marc Bolan, the camp elf, all ermine and feather boa, glitter under his eyes and stars in his hair, being used to sell the ultimate in dull, utilitarian clothing. Funny, no?

Something else that was funny was the thing with Bolan and David Bowie. They'd known each other for years. Both lads on the make, looking for half a chance. They were friends – and rivals. And the pop papers knew it. 'Bowie slams Bolan'. 'Bolan knocks Bowie'. The headlines rattled back and forward. Bowie put a dress on. Bolan sprinkled glitter dust. Bolan broke first, and that just helped Bowie. Maybe that's how it looked in the first year of the Me Decade, but as an impression it lasted about six

NEW ENGLISH LIBRARY

GLAM

Johnny Holland fights to stay idol of a million fans.
By Richard Allen

months. Like Bryan Ferry, Bowie was of the scene, but not really part of it. And he wasn't really interested in it.

If Bolan had invented the scene, Bowie took it, ran around with it for a bit and then let it go. An inspired borrower, Bowie would look around to see what was happening – or what was about to happen – and he'd jump on it, invariably doing it bigger and better, improving on it. Androgyny was in the air, so he wore a dress on the cover of *The Man Who Sold The World* in 1971. Glitter was the thing – there was no one who glittered more than Ziggy Stardust in 1972. Looking back now, it's hard to disassociate ourselves from the artist that Bowie has become. In 1972, who knew or suspected the body of

If Bolan had invented the scene, Bowie took it, ran around with it for a bit and then let it go.

work he'd end up with? 'When words like bizarre, outrageous and camp start being bandied around, then the chances are that the talk has turned to David Bowie' said *Top Of The Pops* magazine in 1972. 'In the last year or so, he has become a superstar in every sense of the word. Today he presents some of the most controversial sights and sounds ever witnessed in pop, some of which must surely leave Mrs Mary Whitehouse positively quivering.'

Mrs Mary who? Ask your mum.

I wonder if the positively quivering Mrs Mary Whitehouse had read the interview Bowie gave with the *Melody Maker* on January 22, 1972.

Headlined Oh You Pretty Thing, it began, 'Even though he wasn't wearing silken gowns right out of Liberty, and his long blond hair no longer fell wavily past his shoulders David Bowie was looking yummy.' Not only did he look yummy, he sounded yummy. 'David's present image is to come on like a swishy queen, a gorgeously effeminate boy. He's as camp as a row of tents, with his limp hand. "I'm gay," he says. "and I always have been, even when I was David Jones." But there's a sly jollity about how he says it, a secret smile at the corners of his mouth.' And on it went. And on he went, pushing the boat a little further each time. In terms of influence, there was no one else. He appeared as Ziggy Stardust and everyone had orange hair. He did *Aladdin Sane* and everyone had a ridiculous approximation of that zig-zag thing across their faces. Like Bryan Ferry, he'd create an outfit and then by the time fans had hold of it, he'd be in something else. He'd shock to get a headline and before the ink was dry, he'd do something worse. So he declared 'I'm gay.' All right, dear. That's fine. But then he started going down on Mick Ronson's guitar on stage! They sung with their arms around each other on *Top Of The Pops!*

David always had one eye on the main chance

What's his

In any Teen Rebel's life there are a few pivotal moments that you will remember for ever. Things that would have once made you ask, 'Mum, what's that mean?' But not this time you wouldn't, though, because you knew that this was about you and it was nothing to do with her. It was a Thursday night in August 1972 and, as contractually obligated, I was sat in front of the telly, watching *Top Of The Pops*. Some patronising, hairy git said something about a new group with a new song and I didn't really take it in and then… 'Make me a deal, and make it straight'. Minutes later, my mother came into the lounge and scraped me off the ceiling. Virginia Plain was one of those rare beasts – a debut single that was more a manifesto than a song. It set out Roxy Music's stall in one sublime moment. It was, simply, the perfect song, maybe the

name? *(Virginia Plain)*

best single ever made. What's her name? Virginia Plain.

The man with the voice like melting jelly and eyes to match was Bryan Ferry. Like Bolan, he found himself under the protective wing of David Enthoven. 'Bryan had a complete vision about what he wanted to do,' recalls the former manager. 'They looked extraordinary. It was all about the look and the girls and it was very interesting. He came to us with the complete package and, sadly, I take no credit for that at all. He came in one day with this tape and it was fantastic. It was bizarre and not very many people liked it, to be honest with you. Bryan's tape was completely different.

'It was all about the look and the girls...'

Bryan wearing his Mum's curtains (left). The lads in the band circa 1974 (right), Bryan opting for uniform, 'cos the girls love it...

It was musical, but it was music played by not particularly good musicians. Which made it even more interesting. It was the first Roxy Music album, the same songs, but in demo form.'

Roxy Music was a fabulous creation, like a bird of paradise. They looked like nothing before and they sounded like nothing had ever sounded. They looked magnificent in their plumage, yet they made this music that was emotional and melancholic and touched with beauty. Counterbalance to Ferry in the band was Brian Eno. A confessed non-musician – an unknown concept at the time – Eno was really a sound engineer who played around with the then-embryonic synthesisers, creating sound textures and weird aural imagery. And he looked astonishing, all feathers and glitz. So what influence did he have in all this?

'You've got to realise that Roxy really was Bryan's creation,' according to Enthoven. 'Eno came and he looked wonderful and he did provide this random musical element, but really everything was Bryan.' Everything? 'Bryan didn't tell the band what to wear, he made suggestions, but they each found their own individual style. He might have to told Paul Thompson [drummer] what to wear. But Bryan's influence was the one that everyone copied.

'America didn't understand them at all. They were too ironic. English irony they never understand. They were much more comfortable with David Bowie. He wore a huge cod piece and stuck his cock out and that they understood. If you're a bit subtle it goes over their head.

'It was slightly ironic and before anyone had done that. They presented the Mickie Mosts and the Chinnichaps with a golden opportunity.'

Indeed they did. But like Moses in the Desert of Sinai, they led their people to a wonderland but didn't go in themselves. Bolan got fat and lazy and Bowie killed off his Glam creation, while Ferry's involvement was more an accident of birth than anything of long-term significance. More than anyone, then, it was Bolan's success that paved the way for a host of imitators. You can almost hear the crowds of pretenders and wannabes now, their cries echoing all the way back from 1971: 'What is he? A cherubic munchkin with glitzy clothes, a bit of glitter and these cutesy nursery rhyme pop tunes, nothing else. And look at all the records he's selling! Look at all the dosh he's making, look at all the girls!' Can't you just hear the conversations in a million pubs up and down the land. 'I can do that. What he's doing. I can do that.' So they did.

Put Your Can In The Can, Honey

What was that?

'*Put your can in the can, honey, Do it while you can*'.

Got to do what, exactly?.

Can The Can. What did that mean? Put something *in* something? It was rude, I guessed, but I did't know. If I'd thought any more about Suzi Quatro I'd have exploded.

The first rule of listening to music is that what you think the words are is infinitely more important than what the words actually are. The words you sing to yourself, these are the words you grow up with, and so while it's highly unlikely that Suzi Quatro actually sang 'Put your can in the can, honey, do it while you can', my 14-year-old self did – and that's what counts.

I think I love

Glam music can be broken up into three distinct groups: the Chinnichap merchants, the Teenybops and the Geezers who just happened to be there at the same time – but let's forget about them.

The Chinnichap types – notably The Sweet, Suzi Quatro and Mud – were signed to producer Mickie Most's RAK label and recorded songs written by Nicky Chinn and Mike Chapman. These boys were inspired by the originators visually and spiritually, but in terms of execution they were a million miles away. They were fun, brash and their ambitions didn't extend beyond getting on *TOTP* and getting to sample of few of the fruits of being a Glam pop star.

The Teenybops – This was basically a two horse race between Donny Osmond and David Cassidy. Between them both, they were probably about 15 years old. The Osmonds were a clan of Mormons who first came to prominence on *The Andy Williams Show*. Take away their single Crazy Horses, which was merely funny, and the Osmonds were about as substantial as a Wagon Wheel after it had been dunked in coffee for too long: sickly, gooey and floppy. And those teeth! Teeth you could have filled a graveyard with. The Osmonds became a corporation – every time you turned around, there was another one that looked the same as all the others but had a different name. Donny was the cutie-pie – again, he looked like the others, but was a bit shinier. Really, the Osmonds were just tedious. When they wheeled out Little Jimmy, well, it was the biggest boost to President Brezhnev that you could imagine. 'I'll be your long-haired lover from Liverpool'? Don't think so, pal! If Little Jimmy would have ever shown that greedy, white, pasty, fat face in Liverpool… Then there was Marie. Yes, they had a female version, of course they had a female version. The Osmonds were Stepford popsters. Five little grinning paying-in slips.

David Cassidy was much more acceptable. How can I be sure that he was? After all, we're in a world that's constantly changing (and if that strikes a chord, you're a sad, sad soul). David Cassidy gained his credibility courtesy of his alter ego, Keith Partridge. Ah, *The Partridge Family*.

you

The Partridge Family was an American TV programme, spiritually from the same shop as *The Brady Bunch*. It was smart in that it took the basic BB format and added three teaspoons of *The Monkees* into the mix. An all-American family who were a pop group.

And why was *The Partridge Family* credible? Because Susan Dey was in it, that's why. At the time Susan Dey was considered top tottie action, though one of the distressing consequences about researching this book is that, looking back, she's genuine jailbait. What could she have been? 14? Susan Dey (if the name's familiar it might be because she later found fame and fortune in *LA Law*) had those dreamy far away eyes that just cried 'Come to me, Jeremy, come to me.' I never did. (You think I'm that easy? Get outta here.)

The Partridge Family was rubbish. How can I be sure? Listen, the world might be constantly changing, but it doesn't change that much. You want further proof? Every telly programme from the era has been rehabilitated and freshly announced kitsch and cool. But *The Partridge Family*? Let me throw this name at you. Danny Bonaduce.

Who else was there on the teenybop front? David Essex, a Brit actor with the sparkiest blue eyes who occasionally knocked out truly bizarre pop songs. Rock On was nothing less than a spaced out, dubbed up treatment of an old Fifties rocker's tune. There were also a couple of American toothpaste adverts called The Williams Twins but, I've got to be honest with you, I don't remember them and, odds on, you don't either. So let's forget about them. The Bay City Rollers? No, they were of a different game really. They were post Donny and David and they wore tartan.

The Partridge Family – when Danny the bassist grew up, he would be arrested for attacking a transvestite hooker

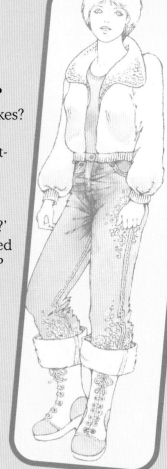

So you wanna be a Glam rocker, kid?

You think you can cut it? You think you've got what it takes? C'm'ere, kid. Let's have a butcher's at your threads. You wanna be a Glam rocker, kid, you gotta have the schmutter. What? You haven't? Listen, you gotta wife? You gotta big sister? You gotta mudda, for Chrissakes? Listen, kid. I got your interests at heart. You wanna make it in this biz, you gotta look the part. Am I right or am I right or am I right?' The man's right. Any self-respecting Glam rocker needed ten basic things. You've got to remember. That first *TOTP* appearance was all-important. Make the right impression and Nicky Chinn and Mike Chapman might take notice. Get it wrong and you're back to doing Beatles and Stones covers at the Greyhound in East Grinstead.

So what was the right look? What were those 10 things?

1) You've got to dress like a girl (or in the case of Suzi Quatro, like a man).

2) You've got to have long hair.

3) Your hair's got to be bouffant.

4) You've got to wear loads of make-up, preferably put on while you're wearing boxing gloves.

5) You've got to wear trousers that are incredibly tight at the top…

6) …And very flared at the bottom.

7) Your trousers have got to be so tight at the top that they split you in two, leaving people in no doubt *a*) about your religion, and *b*) that you're built like a Grand National champion. (The same effect can be achieved by a quick visit to your local greengrocer.)

8) You've got to have loads of glitter and/or mirrors plastered all over you.

9) Your shoes have got to be orthopaedic and be able to double as step-ladders.

10) Any jacket lapels or shirt collars must be at least 6 inches long – and, if you're serious, across.

If you adopted a minimum of, say, five of those points, really, you stood a good chance of making it big. If you did between five and eight, you'd get in the Top 20 after one *TOTP* appearance. If you followed all 10 points, Mickie Most would probably invite you round for dinner.

Basically, the story was this. Think back to when you were very young. Your mother's gone out, there's no one at home and you sneak into her room and you try on her clothes. Listen, don't even bother trying to deny it. We've all done it, boys and girls. You know it's true. Anyway, imagine that you're older. Now do the same thing again. See?

The key in getting dressed, Glam-style, was to forget the idea that you might look a dickhead. You could wear anything you like, any combination of colours or textures. The only thing you couldn't do was look ordinary or normal. Curiously, the clothes tended to look much better if they were really cheap. Tacky, yes, that's obvious. But cheap, that was good too.

Hair was, of course, of supreme importance. It always is.

The key to toptastic hair was this: long at the back and sides, shorter and cut with a curious mix of bouffant and spike on the top. If you could get your hair to hang long at the sides like a cocker spaniels ears, then all the better. It was a wonderfully hideous style which – and this is astonishing – made a comeback among footballers and pop stars in the mid-Eighties. You'd think people would learn, wouldn't you?

The place to go for a cut and blow-dry was Leonard's 'in the heart of London'. The Glitter Band were all patrons of Leonard's, and this is a record of one of their visits: 'Harvey Ellison, who is naturally light brown, had his hair dyed blue. Pete Phipps had his turned a brighter shade of orange. Gerry Shephard decided to go two-tone with the front bright orange and the back dark red. John Rossall had done likewise. John Springate's dark brown hair now sports pale mauve streaks, and, last but not least, Tony Leonard has been dyed blue-black.'

Others preferred a more DIY approach. Brian Connolly's wife took care of his, dishy blond DJ Kid Jensen cut his own and Gary Glitter kept his in the fridge. (Only joking, this was the early Seventies. Gazza's hair was still his own.) Our friends Mud went down Vidal Sassoon's for their barber shop activity.

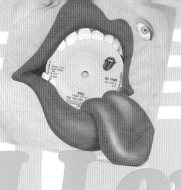

I Love... You

Glam Top Twenty:

1 Blockbuster (1973) The Sweet
2 Rock And Roll, Parts 1 & 2 (1972) Gary Glitter
3 Can The Can (1973) Suzi Quatro
4 Tiger Feet (1974) Mud
5 Get It On (1971) T.Rex
6 Do You Wanna Touch Me (1973) Gary Glitter
7 Jean Genie (1973) David Bowie
8 Ballroom Blitz (1973) The Sweet
9 Merry Xmas Everybody (1973) Slade
10 I'm The Leader Of The Gang (1973) Gary Glitter
11 Hot Love (1972) T.Rex
12 Teenage Rampage (1974) The Sweet
13 Mama Weer All Crazee Now (1972) Slade
14 Starman (1972) David Bowie
15 Virginia Plain (1972) Roxy Music
16 Crazy Horses (1974) The Osmonds
17 Metal Guru (1972) T.Rex
18 Gudbuy T'Jane (1972) Slade
19 Ride A White Swan (1971) T.Rex
20 Cum On Feel The Noize (1973) Slade

Love... Me Love

Where shall we start? Let's start at the very top. Let's start with the biggest and the best, the glitziest and the glammiest, the most toptastic bunch of glamourpusses this side of never: The Sweet.

Blockbusters!

Andy Scott, the lead guitarist said that when The Sweet started out, he used to borrow his wife's make-up. What do you want to know? We can best sum up The Sweet by saying that it probably wasn't a situation that would have lasted too long. How many wives can there have been with a make-up bag to satisfy a man with such a voracious appetite for a bit of red lippy – and the rest? Of all the trash Glam bands, The Sweet were the glammiest. No question. They had the best make-up, the best idiot clothes, the best bouffant nonsense hair, the best pout to the camera – and the best tunes. (We're not including Suzi Quatro in any of this, you understand.)

Maybe the best thing about The Sweet was that they looked like the sort of boys you'd have found in a Birmingham pub knocking out old R&B standards, all sweaty and pints of beer, T-shirts and jeans but, of course, they weren't like that at all.

Formed in 1969 as Wainwright's Gentlemen, they turned into psychedelic bubblegum merchants Sweetshop before dropping the psychedelic (and the 'shop') bit when it went out of fashion… er, I mean when they found their true musical niche.

The Sweet were *the* Glam rock band. Comprising singer Brian Connolly (he of the long blond feather-cut), guitarist Andy Scott, bassist Steve Priest and drummerboy Mick Turner, The Sweet signed to RCA and were the first band to be taken under the protective wings of the songwriting team of

Nicky Chinn and Mike Chapman, and together they pumped out a string of hits: **Funny Funny** (1971), **Co-Co** (1971), **Alexander Graham Bell** (1971), **Poppa Joe** (1972), **Little Willy** (1972), **Wig Wam Bam** (1972), **Blockbuster** (1973), **Hellraiser** (1973), **Ballroom Blitz** (1973) and **Teenage Rampage** (1974).

How many Glam bands (or any other type of bands, for that matter) would have thought of getting a top hit out of a paean to the man who invented the telephone? Not many, surely. The Sweet were crass, playful, absurdly glamorous and curiously macho. There they'd stand on *TOTP* knocking out one of their nonsense, plasticky hits in the Glammest outfits that you could imagine. High-heeled boots, glitzy and satin and glitter and, of course, the tightest trousers you could think of, trousers that made their crotches... well, split in two. Little Willy? Not bloody likely, pal.

For the first few years, they were tat. The songs were tat, plastic, horrible manufactured tat. They looked and sounded like puppy fat. Put them next to the likes of Chicory Tip and you'd have been pushed hard to see the difference.

And then something happened.

They suddenly became overt. In 1972, Mecca banned them from playing concerts in their clubs because of their 'sexually overt stage act'. Infamy assured, they went on to be one of the genre's only real supergroups.

They sold 50 million records and at their height lived the rock 'n' roll life to the full. Notorious consumers of things to make you feel good, they burned. Connolly typified their excess, buying a huge mansion in Surrey, a £250,000 yacht and employing a full-time gardener, maid and chauffeur.

In December 1974, The Sweet had a brainwave – something that's generally not a good idea for anyone. It's something that's definitely never a good idea for a pop group.

They decided to split from Chinn and Chapman and write their own songs. They'd rumbled about doing something like this before. They'd written their own b-sides in the past and, in an effort to placate them, Chinn and Chapman had altered their writing style. Suddenly, their songs rocked. That run of four songs from Blockbuster to Teenage Rampage, that's a body of work that you'd be proud of. It was like an overnight conversion. Really, it went from you the viewer being embarrassed when they were on *TOTP* to sitting there, hoping, praying that they'd be on.

One of the first fruits of that was the crackin', zingin' Blockbuster with its sirens and rockin' guitar and Jean Genie riff. Blockbuster was THE SONG. Blockbuster should have been adopted as the national anthem. (The idea of The Queen turning to the camera, pouting and 'We just haven't got a clue what to do' – it's too delicious for words.)

Blockbuster was like… Every generation has its song. Rock Around The Clock, Anarchy In The UK, Fool's Gold, Blockbuster. Honest, it was that good. Really, and I don't mean any disrespect here, but The Sweet should have died in a plane crash after Blockbuster. If they'd taken the smart career move, Athena would never have finished the poster print run. The musical would never have left the West End. Listen, they can make a musical out of *Buddy*, some geek in glasses, think of what they could have done with The Sweet.

The thing with Blockbuster was that it was the (and I'm sorry for this) zeitgeist. It was exactly the right song at exactly the right time. Bolan's Ride A White Swan might have been more iconoclastic, Bowie's Ziggy trip might have been more dramatic, Roxy's Virginia Plain might have been the best debut single ever (before or since) but Blockbuster… It was like you need a pint of milk so you go to a pint of milk shop and buy a pint of milk. We needed Blockbuster and, right on time, there she was.

That upped the ante all right, and Chinn and Chapman rose to the challenge. Next up was Ballroom Blitz with its comical Joan Crawford opening – Brian inquiring 'Are you ready, Steve?... Are you ready Mick?...Are you ready Andy?...Well, let's goooooo' and Hellraiser. How many dance-floors rocked to the sound of The Sweet? How many times did you hear that air raid siren that welcomed in Blockbuster and rush to the dancefloor? (Well, rush as well as you could in five-inch heels).

And then...

'We're proper musicians... we're creative artistes... wanna do our own stuff...'

Yeah, and record it on Dobly.

And that, really, was the end of The Sweet. At least it is as far as we're concerned. OK, so they scored with Fox On The Run in 1975, but the hits dried up as they sought to – and it kills me to write this – gain acceptance as proper musicians. They went to America and tried to reincarnate as a heavy metal group, but mostly they ended up playing the rock star and taking advantage of all things that life has to offer a young rock star. To be fair, they had a modicum of success, but there was a hint of 'taking coals to Newcastle' about it all. They had a sort of success by proxy through Kiss who ripped off their songs and look and attitude, turned the volume up to 11 and, naturally, made a fortune.

The Sweet started life as a comical bubblegum group doing comical pop songs – really, Little Willy? – and ended life as a bunch of old bickering sadsters, but for a brief, glorious period they burned brighter than bright and were the starriest star in the sky. That should be enough for anyone. Fittingly, when they blew up, they blew up big time and the whole thing ended in bitter acrimony – alcohol, arguments and early death – not the sort of thing we need go into here. You want to know about all that, go find a Sweet biography. Later, Steve Priest said: 'We were drinking too much and taking too many drugs – which seemed to be a good idea at the time.' I'm sure it did Steve. But it wasn't.

Remember them this way. It's 1973 and The Sweet are on *TOTP* performing Blockbuster. The camera closes in on Steve Priest, who's wearing so much make-up that Boots had to create a new range just for him, he turns and mouths the classic Glam aside – 'We just haven't got a clue *what* to do.' It was so camp you could have put it in a field and slept in it.

Perfect ☆☆

WIG WAM BAM
The Final Words of Brian Connolly

Tragically, **Brian Connolly,** Sweet's blond, athletic, swaggering front man, died in 1997. When we met in the bizarre setting of his modern detached home, stripped of all fittings and furnishings, in Denham Village, Uxbridge, in 1993, 25 years of rock 'n' roll excess had been deeply etched into his welcoming face. Nevertheless, slumped in the shadows of a corner of the living room, his former swagger seemed to return as he spoke with enthusiasm and eloquence.

'Glam was always coming for me. Glam. It was showbiz. It was always there. Right back when I was a little kid, in Glasgow, all the neighbours would congregate in each others houses and have sing-songs. I'd always do my turn… honestly, I'd make a show of it. I'd put my mother's hats on… anything to stand out. That's all it was, standing out from the rest. I even used this tactic at Glasgow Barrowlands when I won a country and western singing competition.

'The Sweet started in London. I was living in Uxbridge in the Sixties, singing in skiffle bands and things. I replaced Ian Gillan in a soul band called Wainwright's Children. I remember they kicked out their drummer, Mick, because he was, er, flamboyant. I liked him. I liked his style. He had a showbizzy approach and that seemed much more fun.

'So I left and teamed up with him.

'We were called Sweetshop at first. We were into The Doors and Buffalo Springfield but delivered those influences in a poppy kind of way. We were almost identical to Marmalade but, at a BBC session, we met up with these two songwriters, Chinn and Chapman.

'The dressing up was the most fun I'd ever had. Then, when you are known for producing singles like Little Willy and Funny Funny, nothing really matters anymore. We just didn't care. It was success at all costs and, if it meant that we lost a bit of artistic satisfaction… well, that was tough. We knew how good we could be. Those early singles were just cynical stabs at getting into the charts and we were happy with that. And if we hadn't done them, we'd probably still

be trudging around the pub circuit now. Anyway, we didn't give a damn what some idiots at the *Melody Maker* might think. We weren't doing it for them. It wasn't their career at stake, was it? So we wondered, how could we take this a stage further? How could we really go out on a limb? Dead simple. Like me in me old mum's house, we'd dress up. Like crazy. This doesn't seem particularly outrageous now, people wear what they want, today. But you must remember, this was the early Seventies. There were still a number of taboos to be broken and a load of big guys wearing make-up was certainly one of them. The reaction, the sheer vehemence against us was quite extraordinary. People wanted to kill us. Even though it was obvious that it was all just a gimmick… a bit of fun. People genuinely wanted to kill us. And if it wasn't the ordinary working class men who, for some reason, felt threatened, then it was the hard rock fans who accused us of selling out. That was a laugh. How can you accuse a band who sang Little Willy of selling out? Anyway, I didn't believe in all that rock snobbery stuff. The fact is we were honest about it. We weren't selling out any more than half those dull underground bands. They would have killed for the exposure we got.

'We did tend to shock people. Much more than Gary Glitter or Bowie or Bolan, for some reason. We were a little bit like the punk groups. I certainly knew how they felt when people reacted against them and I was really proud when The Damned did Ballroom Blitz. But it wasn't a way of life for us. We were always a rock band at heart. Glam was just a tag that came along and we rode with it, shamelessly. But you can hear that lack of shame in the records, and the records were great.

'I know there wasn't a lot of camaraderie between the bands. We got on all right with everyone, but it wasn't like, all the glammy bands would get together. There was no sense of a movement, so it wasn't like punk at all. In fact, it was a pretty sordid scramble just to get hits. But that's what was so good about it. It was so honest. If anything, any sense of belonging came afterwards, much later, in the late Eighties, actually, when everyone suddenly became interested in the Seventies again. We are friendly with the guys from Mud today, for example. We tour with them. To be honest, I don't think we ever spoke to them at the time. In fact, if you really want me to be honest, I can actually remember us walking straight past Mud in the corridor at the BBC. We didn't acknowledge them and they didn't look at us. Yes, Les is a great mate now, but not then. Glam was something that came out of everyone's rehearsals sessions and their meetings with their own managers. We would watch the other bands like hawks and they'd watch us. So we'd all be planning what to wear, getting increasingly outrageous, trying to out-shock the other bands. I remember someone from Mud being really angry because Showaddywaddy had these really bright-coloured drape jackets while theirs were pale grey or blue. Next time Mud were on they had day glo drape jackets, and so on. We were as bad. Whatever Dave Hill wore we'd copy and then go one stage more, then he'd see us and take it even further.

'I wouldn't say all that scramble to be more Glam than the next band was a bad thing. It must have been great fun for the fans, who'd be at home, spraying their platforms silver. Someone told me recently that we had a gang of golden skinheads following us around. I don't remember them at all but apparently they'd turn up at our gigs and would be completely sprayed gold – hair, faces, clothes, braces, Doc Martens, the lot. I wish I'd seen them. They must have looked stunning.

'At the time, though, to be honest, we were only really interested in ourselves. We were a bit selfish. But Glam was good for the music because our singles, I thought, got better and better. By the time we were doing The Six Teens the Glam thing may have faded but we were really making the music that we always knew we could make. And it was Glam that pushed us through to that level. A hell of a long way from Little Willy.

'My favourite artists? Bowie, of course. Doors. Led Zeppelin. All the Glam bands were into Led Zeppelin and Deep Purple, strangely enough. I had a secret soft spot for Black Sabbath, who used to get this real progressive rock audience but, when you think about it, Ozzy and the lads were pretty much a Glam thing. And Alice Cooper, of course. He was another one who managed to get a more serious audience and he was pure showbiz. Nice guy, too, and a massive fan of The Sweet. He tried to help us in America. Funny, that. America. For ages we were known for Little Willy which, for some reason, was a million-seller over there. Blockbuster didn't really work in America. I think maybe it was a very British kind of record. Blockbuster was a kind of get drunk and go to the football kind of song. That said, Ballroom Blitz was a big US hit, though. In America you didn't have the same kind of snobbishness. Glam was just part of rock. If I hadn't drunk so much I could tell you a lot more about America. But it's all a haze. Happened so fast, too. Great times. I think. Hahaaa!

The Cat Crept In

Mud. **What do you want** to know about Mud? This will give you a bit of an idea about Mud. While researching this book, I interviewed Pan's People – it's a tough job, isn't it? – and we were talking about life at *TOTP* and what the backstage story was and so on. So I said, 'Which group was the best laugh, the least pretentious, the least full of themselves?' After about maybe half a second, they said in one voice, 'Mud.'

Formed in the early Seventies, Mud bumbled along for a bit before being taken under the wing of RAK and the Midas-like Chinn and Chapman songwriting partnership. They'd done wonders for The Sweet, what could they do for Mud? In 1972, RAK and Mud was a partnership made in heaven. RAK was interested in scoring hits, Mud were interested in being on *TOTP* and having a laugh. The partnership suited both sides and it worked a treat. They scored a total of 15 hits between 1972 and 1976 and the tigertastic Tiger Feet was top of the charts for six glorious weeks in 1973. There was, however, a cloud on the horizon: they wrote their own b-sides. But that was for the future. In the Glam-orous early Seventies, Mud knew where they stood. 'We owe so much to the faith that Nicky, Mike and Mickey had in us at the very start. We were virtually an unknown group when we met them,' said Les. Now I don't know this, but I suspect that Mud even made the Xmas single, Lonely This Christmas, a melodramatic slice of kitsch nonsense.

The best of the chancers, Mud were The Damned of the class of '73. In it for the crack and not a lot else. Have a laugh, a bit of a giggle – and out. But it got a bit carried away with itself and Les Gray, Dave Stiles, Rob Davies and Dave Mount found that they were a bit more popular than I suspect they ever figured

they would be. And that's fine by us, because apart from anything else it meant that Mud didn't commit the cardinal sin. Les with his snug white lurex trousers, effeminate Rob with his cack-handed make-up and his mother's dresses and the two Daves doing what Daves do best: drink and play pool.

'We used to enjoy the rock 'n' roll lifestyle on the road,' said Big Les wistfully later. 'We never got into the drugs thing, but there was plenty of boozing, partying and clubbing. It was great fun.'

Mud were so of their time that life as a long-term career was never an option, and after the Glam bubble burst in 1976, they disappeared, jettisoned by their public like an empty fuel tank. Sir Les kept going after the others left, renaming the band… Les Gray's Mud and hitting the chicken-in-a-basket circuit. It was all too reminiscent of The Sweet – who suddenly and silently became Brian Connolly's Sweet.

Les Gray's Mud continued touring until 1997 when ill health tapped him on the shoulder – a bill from the early Seventies. Now 52 and living in Portugal, Les no longer wears white lurex trousers. 'My missus decided to clear out an old wardrobe and gave the lot to Oxfam. There's probably someone walking around west London wearing all my stuff even now,' he said not so long ago.

Before Les's illness stopped play, the highlight of Les Gray's Mud calendar was the annual pop festival they played with fellow revivalists Showaddywaddy in Denmark at a place called Legoland. There's not a lot you can say to that.

THAT'S NEAT, THAT'S NEAT, THAT'S NEAT...
Les Gray in his Tiger Feet

Mud vocalist **Les Gray,** who always looked slightly out of time, like a Teddy Boy at a Seventies wedding, speaks from his Portuguese retreat where apparently, he sips red wine, sits by a raging log fire and dreams of long lost days of Glam.

'Well, it was just mad, wasn't it? Anything went in those days. Yes, yes. We were a product of Chinn and Chapman. I remember when Mike Chapman first showed me the lyrics to Tiger Feet. I mean, can youimagine? I just fell about laughing. I said. "I'm not singing thaaat! You've got to be joking, mate." I mean, think about it. You are in a pop band, you've had a few hits and, even if only for our guitarist, Rob, the girls are beginning to assemble where you go, you just start to take yourself a little seriously and then this guy wants you to sing Tiger Feet! "Bugger off!" I thought. I mean, what would you think?

'I'll never forget the first time we rehearsed that song. I just couldn't stop laughing… literally fell over in stitches. I just thought that song would really blow it for us. It was so stupid. I couldn't see it being a hit. I knew everyone would laugh at it. But look what happened. It just caught the right moment. The song seemed to be just what the DJs were looking for. It got people packing onto the dance floor, all doing that silly dance. The Mud dance. We nicked that from the old Shadows routine. We went back to Mike Chapman after we had messed about with his song and come up with that dance and he knew instantly how big it would be.

'We didn't really have any style. There was nothing Glam about us, at first. We were a bit like Showaddywaddy in image. Drape jackets in bright Seventies colours. We didn't have a clue about clothes, really, or that we might be perceived as Glam. They were just stage clothes. Things started to take off when Rob (Davis) started wearing his little jackets and those massive flares. That was simply because he was too skinny for the drape look. He'd look stupid. So we draped him in scarves and all those things…like leopard skin bell-bottoms.

'Gradually people started making him clothes and he became known for being the outrageous one, which he wasn't, really. But all the girls would be camping outside the gates of his house and everything. It became a bit wild. We had big problems with his dad over that when Rob started wearing making-up and getting really Glam. His dad went completely bonkers. He said, "What have you done to my son? What have you turned him into?" Rob had a lot of tabloid exposure in 1974, which was great for us. We were just enjoying it for what it was. It wasn't serious. We didn't hang out with any of the other bands. The parties we had were just with our own mates. The bands never spoke to each other. In the Nineties, when we started doing revival tours, I became big mates with Brian (Connolly) but I would never have never spoken to him back then. We'd turn up, do *Top Of The Pops* and get out. We didn't want to know how good the other guys were. The competition was furious and that is what made everyone start dressing up in a more and more outrageous manner.

Cum On Feel

Slade started life as **Ambrose Slade,** a bunch of threatening skins from Walsall. By 1971, they'd lost the Ambrose and Noddy Holder was giving it loads on *TOTP* with this top hat covered in mirrors. 'The first time it was for a stage effect,' said Noddy. 'I wanted it to be like a mirror ball and light up the audience. But I ended up wearing it for two years, 1972 and 1973. The idea was that when we went on *TOTP* we wanted to stand out. We wanted people to say in the pub, "Did you see them Slade on *Top Of The Pops* last night? They're mad, they are".'

As ambitions go, that was a fair ambition. The only thing was that Slade weren't mad. They were sharp tunesmiths who had a gift for a gag and an eye for the main chance.

First spotted by Chas Chandler, a man who'd proved his pedigree with his previous managerial charge, one Jimi Hendrix. When Chandler got hold of Slade, they were still Ambrose Slade and about to become skins. In the very late Sixties being a skin was quite a smart move. It was a big constituency, ready to be exploited, but when they got going they found that they weren't the ones being exploited. Skins used their gigs to launch all that violence nonsense that they liked so much. Every time the Ambroses tried to get going, out would come the DMs and the knuckle-dusters. For a young group on the make, it wasn't so much a reputation as a noose. 'Hey, we're better than that,' thought the boys. So they lost the Ambrose, grew their hair and had a look around. 'Hey, who's that bunch of poofs singing about that geezer wot invented the phone?'

It didn't take long for the shrewd Chandler to reposition his boys as Glam rockers and, hey ho, here we go, they released Get Down And Get With It, a good old stomp from their old days that was now dressed up with a bit of fairy dust. It was, strangely enough, a Top 20 hit.

The Noize

Noddy Holder, the lead singer and the owner of that mirrored top hat, was so pleased he wrote a letter to his mum. 'Deer mum, Gess wot weev dun...' Chas Chandler happened to be passing by as Noddy was writing and saw the letter. 'Oi, Nod, I think I've got an idea.'

Well, it might have been like that.

Slade had themselves a gimmick. It was to pretend that they hadn't been to skool. They spelt all their song titles wrong. **Coz I Luv You**, **Look Wot You Dun**, **Take Me Bak 'Ome**, **Mama Weer All Crazee Now**, **Gudbye T'Jane**, **Cum On Feel The Noize**... Slade had a huge run of hits. Each time they appeared on *TOTP*, they were more and more outrageous. Or rather, guitarist Dave Hill was. One of the great Glam figures, Hill looked like no one else on earth: huge platform boots – I've a sneaky suspicion he was about four foot tall – costumes to dye for in colours to die in, the trademark Cleopatra haircut and the cutest buck teeth. That haircut was the crowning glory. Long all round, except at the front where it was cut in a kind of round circle. It was well odd. He looked like a comical posh chipmunk who'd been off nicking peanuts when they were giving out good taste. A proper job Glam Liberace, Hill was a permanent fixture of the early Seventies.

Sparkling hair and glamtastic clothes alone wouldn't have done it for the Sladesters. Their tunes were catchy, rocky, infectious, so much so that they're still living. A rabble-rousing leader of a rabble-rousing outfit, Noddy Holder's voice was a raspy growl, obviously the perfect voice for an effeminate-looking (oh yeah?) Glam rock outfit. Like The Sweet, Slade made some timeless classics. And like The Sweet their look seemed totally at odds with what they were. Coming from the Black Country of Wolverhampton – Black Sabbath country – it was only natural that their tendency should be toward the macho, but you just felt with Slade that half a yard underneath the bucket loads of glitter there were two tattoos that said 'love' and 'hate'. Maybe it was their skin background.

What happened to Slade? They got soft. They started making proper records. They learned to spel. They got ideas. They made a film – *Flame*, aka *Slade In Flame* – that was all soft focus and backlit. Listen, if *Slade In Flame* had been a kosher item, it would have been called *Slade In Flaym*. You want to know another reason we got bored with Slade? Merry Xmas Everybody. More a pension scheme than a record, it has lurked around our consciousness for what? Twenty-five years?

The Sweet. Mud. Slade. Each was pivotal and that era we call Glam would have been a poorer place without them. They all flirted in that nether zone somewhere between proper pop group and cartoon pastiche. They enjoyed playing and we enjoyed watching them play and it was all a bit of a gag, but… The Sweet wanted to be proper rock stars, Mud toyed with it, writing their own b-sides, Slade, if the truth be told, were a proper pop group. There was a place in our hearts – and in the market – for a group, for something that had absolutely no pretensions to being proper. The teenybops had no pretensions but that was something completely different. What we're talking about here is something that was a cartoon.

But real.

TAKE ME BAK 'OME
OK, says Noddy Holder

Everybody loved Slade. Even prog rock dullards allowed a foot to tap to *Mama Weer All Crazee Now*. There really wasn't any point in disliking them. Everyone knew they were one of the most ferocious live rock acts on the planet. (Indeed, most of the prog rock fans had been totally duped by Slade, after purchasing, and subsequently worshipping, their pre-Glam *Slade Alive* album). What's more, they were just profoundly unpretentious Brummies grabbing their chance. This almost universal fondness seems to remain intact, and has even survived the eternal annual recycling of Merry Xmas Everybody. If we can forgive that, we can forgive anything.

'Drives me mad, that song. Let alone anyone else. It's a great song really but…sorry world. Didn't mean it. It were just a bit of Christmas fun, not supposed to last 26 years – and counting.

'Glam! Where did that come from? We were managed by Chas Chandler and we'd done the progressive rock circuit for some time. He'd turn up and look at us and he'd be thinking, "This lot look just the same as all the other progressive rock bands." And he was right. We looked and sounded no different than a thousand other bands. It seemed hopeless. I think Chas had this vision of making us appeal to the younger brothers of the progressive people. It had all got stuck in a post-hippy rut, so he told us to shave all our hair off. He'd seen all these kids running around London, skinheads, so he reasoned we'd make a good skinhead band.

'The first skinhead band. It wasn't real. Me and Don weren't too bothered but it was never really Dave. He hated it. But we were skinheads for a while. We got a lot of press out of it but I don't think the skinheads actually ever liked us. They were into reggae.

'They wanted Prince Buster, not some Brummie idiots. So we just sort of grew our hair. This is where the Glam thing started. For some reason, Dave grew his hair long at the sides but kept that short Cleopatra look on top, which was pretty strange. My hair was short on top. I think we noticed Marc Bolan – with Tyrannosaurus Rex, probably – and he was beginning to sprinkle himself with glitter, so we had a go. Dave was the first Glam member of Slade and it always suited him better than me, Jim or Don, 'cause we always just looked like blokes. There was no way we could look any other way. But Dave was spraying his long coat silver. He had a silver leather jacket which really looked great. And then came the platforms... We have to give a lot of credit to Chas. We would probably have spent a dull career making endless concept albums if it wasn't for him. He encouraged us to write short little pop songs. We didn't have a clue. Me and Jim knocked up Cos I Luv You in about 10 minutes. People now say that it's a beacon of the Glam age. We were just messing around and suddenly it became this massive hit. But I couldn't figure it out. It was like being put on a roller coaster because for the next few years things would just happen. We were four mates, having a laugh, really drinking hard – and I mean hard – and everything we wrote turned to gold. Even bad things, like having to fulfil a whole string of small pre-booked venues after we had a number one hit, worked in our favour. We were playing pubs and there would be queues of 5,000 people outside. It made the headlines and made us seem much bigger than we really were. It wasn't clever or planned. It all just happened that way.

'People liked us because we were so ordinary. Alright, so we had daft clothes, but everyone knew we put ketchup on our chips, if you catch my drift. A lot of our new-found fans were very young. A 16-year-old lad with his 15-year-old girlfriend. They would like Slade and Motown. They would play our singles at parties. It wasn't a serious thing, like sitting down in your bedroom smoking dope and scrutinising the lyrics. It was just a laugh. We got into a bit of bother over the misspellings. But I thought that was ridiculous, so patronising for the kids. They understood the joke alright. They were intelligent enough to know that Skweeze Me Pleeze Me wasn't spelt right. Those kids were a lot brighter than people would think.

'Someone said that Gary Glitter chose his name after seeing Dave Hill on *Top Of The Pops*. I don't know about that but we were pretty early onto it. It felt like fun right from the start. Cos I Luv You crashed in at number one in 1971. That's surprisingly early, isn't it? I know that The Sweet and Chinnichap came to a Slade gig to check us out just before their big change. That must have been a bit confusing for them because they were a rock band who had had to lighten up a lot to get hits. Now they saw us and we were probably rocking pretty hard at that point. Yeah, must have been odd. But that Glam thing was very rocky, wasn't it?

'It would be wrong for us to say that it was one long party because it was anything but. Most of the time we would be doing nothing at all. Like any successful band, we'd be pacing around hotel rooms and I hated it.

'It was funny. It was like you lived in a life that was, for 23 hours of the day, more boring than a normal life. Hanging around airports, hotels, in cars, coaches. Then you'd get an hour of madness and then back to the tedium. During our peak, during the Glam years, it was like living in this grey world and then suddenly being unleashed into this fantastically colourful, glittery one, and then slipping back into the grey. As if Glam was some kind of parallel universe. I exaggerate a bit but there were times when that's how it seemed. We never really saw the other bands. A lot of it came out in the film *Slade In Flame*, which, although fictitious was very true to life. The director, Andrew Birkin – brother of Jane – came on the road with us in America to see what it was like. He picked up on that band dynamic, brilliantly.

Come On Come

It was an invitation that was almost impossible to reject. Who wouldn't wanna be in his gang?

Gary **Glitter was the name,** taking the piss was the game. To try to describe Gary Glitter physically... I can't come near to doing it justice. Listen, if Shakespeare, Chaucer and that bloke what wrote The Bible sat down together and tried, they couldn't come near to doing it justice.

Gary Glitter stared down from the *TOTP* stage in 1972, dressed in this top-to-toe Bacofoil outfit – top-to-toe. The top bit was undone halfway down his chest, revealing what can only be described as a carpet. Never had chest hair been so celebrated. And it was podgy. The words 'Christmas' and 'turkey' came to mind. The toe bit was encased in these silver platform boots that were...well, they were architectural. People lived in them. At the height of the property boom, a one-bed flat in the heel of one of Gary's boots went for £125,000. His hair was this huge thatch that sat on top of his head, almost as though it had been placed there. His eyes were wide and wild, but they weren't wide and wild like he was mad and they weren't wide and wild like he was on drugs. They were wide and wild out of shock, the shock of being where he was, looking like he was, doing what he was. And there he stood. Or rather, and there he stood, wobbling. Perched atop a high-rise block of council flats, he couldn't dance – he couldn't actually move (can you imagine the leg muscles that he'd have needed? Steve Austin himself would have struggled) – so he wobbled. And as he wobbled

Come On

On Come On

he waved his arms around, maybe because that was the only part of his body that he could move, more likely because he was in danger of falling off his boots and he was trying to retain a sense of balance. Balance! What an odd word to use here.

The song that he was there to promote, it was like nothing anyone had ever heard. Not so much a song as a chant, it was a repetitive beat backed by this great thumping thudding noise that was generated by not one but two drummers, each of whom seemed to know nothing of the finer points of drumming. 'Here, this is the stick and that's the drum and you hit that with that and that's about it.' Over the top of this beat thing was this fuzzy guitar that knocked out something that was more rhythm than melody, but it passed as the melody because there was nothing else. And that was it. Every so often, Gary would give a particularly violent wobble, throw his arms out and make his eyes even wider and wilder and shout 'Hey!' And that was it. And – and in many way this is the crowning glory – they called it Rock 'n' Roll Parts 1 & 2.

Gary was backed by, obviously, The Glitter Band, a similarly-bedecked mob who looked like normal versions of him. The guitarist had a guitar that was shaped like a star. And when Gary threw out his arms and went 'Hey!' they too threw out their arms and went 'Hey!'

It was a performance that, had it happened 60 years earlier, would have been hailed as a great Dadaist triumph. The Futurists would have claimed Gary as their own. If he had appeared in the Eighties, Gary would have been a concept designed by the creatives at some Thatcherite advertising agency. If he'd have appeared in the Nineties, Gary would have been not simply a post-modern deconstruction, but an ironic post-modern deconstruction.

Whatever it was, it was what it was. Rock 'n' Roll Parts 1 & 2 made Gary Glitter a star overnight. It was fantastic disco music. I can remember (OK, vaguely remember) dancing in the local disco to this thing and it was great.

Come On...

What a question. What a thing to ask. But, funnily, it didn't seem at all sexual.

I mean,

'Do you wanna touch me...

(where?)

There!'

(Nowadays of course, it has a sinister undertone. But that's only with hindsight)

It was like an aural spinning mirror ball. Boom da boom boom, boom da boom! Boom da boom boom, boom da boom – Hey! It came as no surprise to learn that Rock 'n' Roll Parts 1 & 2 had been a big dancefloor filler in discos up and down the land for months before Gary appeared out of the mists that Thursday evening on *TOTP*.

A proper job showman, Gary Glitter wasn't so much a pop star as a music hall variety act. And as he got more successful – and he got very successful – he got more and more music hall. 'I'm most of all, I suppose, an entertainer,' he said at the time. Like, what else is he going to be?

Not everyone got it. The *Top Of The Pops Annual* for 1974 said: 'The singing is plainly repetitive, some say monotonous and is not entirely pleasing. Often, he seems to be playing the same song over and over, but nobody seems to notice. In fact, the more he sings a song, the more people appear to like it.' The more people appear to like it. That's a statement.

While his songwriting partner Mike Leander stayed put behind the scenes, Gary Glitter knocked out hit after hit after hit, touching a genuine populist nerve. The kids loved him because he was all glittery and fun and the music was great. The mums and dads also loved him because he was all glittery and fun and the music was great. Gary reminded them of when they used to go out to places like the Moss Empires. Wilson, Keppel and Betty. Gary Glitter. What was he if not a sand dance?

The hits? **I Didn't Know I Loved You Till I Saw You Rock 'n' Roll**, **Hello, Hello**, **I Love You Love Me Love**, **Do You Wanna Touch Me?**, **I'm The Leader Of The Gang**. The thing is, it was genuinely funny. Gary Glitter standing there – and apart from getting a bit porkier and exaggerating everything, he never did change the act from the one he did that first time on *TOTP*, wobbling and throwing his arms around and asking, 'Do you wanna touch?' over and over again, remembering to never physically point to where. If it had been anyone else, the BBC wouldn't have let it through. They would have said it was obscene or filthy or something. But it was Gary and obscene really didn't come into it. Not then, anyway. Later is a different computer hard disk altogether.

Then, when he started his Leader Of The Gang schtick – 'Do you wanna be in my gang, my gang, my gang?' proclaiming himself as the leader of the gang. I mean, really. Can you imagine being in Gary's gang? But everyone did and everyone said 'Yes' and soon enough Gary was being called simply The Leader. In anyone else's hands this wouldn't have gone down well. The Leader. We don't like that sort of thing here. But it was Gary so it was OK. Anyway, the idea of Gary Glitter harbouring some sort of fascist fantasy…

Like all overnight stars, there was a lot more to Gary Glitter than met the eye. His life is a real showbiz story. Illegitimate, in and out of children's homes…all that. He was 27 when Rock 'n' Roll, Parts 1 & 2 hit gold, old by glitterpop standards – and, incidentally, he brilliantly turned that to his advantage too, using it to make him appear even more of a cartoon: not only does he look like he looks, but he's an old git to boot! – and he'd been around the block a fair few times already. Born Paul Gadd, he'd already reinvented himself once, releasing nine singles as Paul Raven. It didn't work and he kept the wolf from the door by doing things like *Jesus Christ Superstar*. Donkey work. He became Paul Monday. Then Rubber Bucket (don't ask) before he finally became Gary. When Gary Glitter hit big, he didn't only hit big as a parody of a rock star, he lived his life that way as well. A huge mansion, Rolls-Royce and – get this – an octagonal bed with a built-in fridge, the door of which opened automatically when the champagne was at just the perfect temperature.

Gary Glitter. Apparently it could have been Terry Tinsel. When Glam rock died, Gary Glitter hit a trough of despair and descended into the usual rock star abyss. (It's strange how there are some things you just cannot parody.) Then he had a brainwave. Those kids who came to see me in the early Seventies, they're all grown up now. They're old enough to be students. And so Gary set off in his scaled down Roller – a Cortina – and reinvented himself as a kitsch icon. The thing is, he always was.

Drink and drugs, best friendship with Keith Moon, bankruptcy, the Revenue, the Long Arm… And through it all the Great British Public loved him. He became an icon, a Character. The more that he did, the more the Brits loved him. It got to the stage where you wondered what he'd have to do to get people to turn against him…

Coo Coo,

he Engelbert to Gary's Tom Jones was Alvin Stardust. He hadn't always been Alvin Stardust. In all truth, there was no Mr and Mrs Stardust. But then again, I don't suppose there was a Mr and Mrs Glitter. Still. Born Bernard Jewry, at 16 he became Shane Fenton. 'But I've been Alvin for longer than either of them and it seems silly to change,' he said in the 1990s. I suppose it's true. What's your true name? The name that your parent gave you or the name that everybody knows you by? 'I was gonna be Elvin – like Elvis – and Star – like Ringo Starr. But somehow what came out was Alvin Stardust. I blame Gary Glitter. I was just cashing in on his Glam-rock bit and having a bit of fun.'

After a brief burst of success as Fenton, Alvin (or Shane, as he still was) crossed to the other side of the shop and went into management, looking after The Hollies and Lulu, among others. But what fun is it, watching other people get all the fame and accolades? There was only one thing for it. He put down the phone and set about reinventing himself.

Glam was the perfect world to unveil a new you and Shane's new him was a treat. Alvin Stardust burst forth like a butterfly breaking out of its larval stage. Tight black leather jeans, tight black leather top, tight black leather gloves… It didn't bear thinking about what else was tight and wrapped in black leather. The shirt/jacket was undone, revealing a satanic-looking upside-down cross. He wore huge rings – on the outside of his gloves. He had a quiff the size of the Eiffel Tower and sideburns like some Amazonian forest. And he never, ever, ever smiled.

It was a very comical front. Just the thing of a threatening, mean and moody black leather rock God called Alvin. It was a hoot. The perfect counterpoint to the boy Glitter. His first record, My Coo Ca Choo, was a

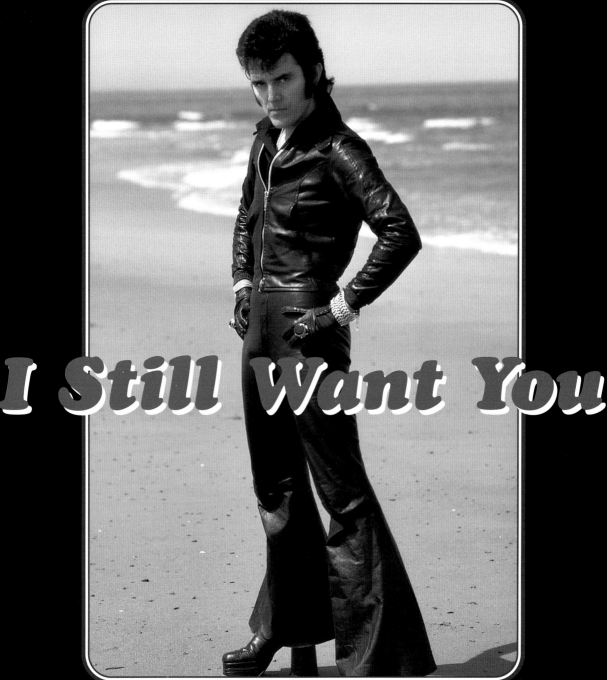

huge hit. One appearance on *TOTP*, that's all it took and for the first time in his life, Bernard Jewry was a star. After that, it was easy. Between 1973 and 1985, Alvin had 13 hits – and if you can name more than one of them, give me a bell.

These days, he does revue shows with The Glitter Band and Mud called

Aside from the drink, the drugs, the bankruptcy, the Bacofoil, the Revenue grief, the post-ironic career resurrection, the bit about being a Great British Character, an icon and the syrup, Alvin was exactly the same as Gary. They're like Captain Scarlet and Captain Black.

things like The Solid Silver Seventies. 'I've made a living at this for 30 years and all I want people to do is laugh along with me.' That seems quite reasonable to me.

There were others. Everywhere you looked, there were others.

The third member of the Chinn and Chapman stable was Suzi Quatro. Like your man Alvin, Suzi went down the 'I'm a rocker, me' route. All black leather and no smile, diminutive Suzi stood there pouting and preening while her outsize guitarist – hubbie Len Tuckley – stood towering over her, like a watchful bouncer keeping an eye out. Together with her 'hard-hitting' band, Suzi was a permanent fixture on *TOTP* in the early Seventies.

Can The Can.

That was Suzi, number one, March 1973. There was also **48 Crash** (July 1973), **Daytona Demon** (October 1973), **Devil Gate Drive** (February 1974) and... er... Suzi kind of ran out of petrol after that. There were a couple of other hitettes, nothing much to speak of. But we loved Suzi. It wasn't a sexual thing – Big Len was standing there. What could anyone have done? It was just that she was, well, sweet.

'Put your can in the can, honey.' I mean, how couldn't you?

Elton John – yes, the same one who now makes a living singing about...no, better not say that, it's near blasphemous. Elton was a way-over-the-top Glamster who could glitter with the best of them and had his very own trademark – his outrageous specs. Huge, colourful, ridiculous spectacles. Elton's glasses had lights attached, windscreen wipers, fans... Elton was always making a spectacle of himself! Elton first lodged himself in the public consciousness during the Glam era. Big platform boots – and we mean big – outrageous costumes and a complete lack of fear. Look a prat? Don't care. Elton was a showman and would have come on the Glam boy in any era. More than that, though, the reason that we don't really care about Elton John is this: he was dull as dishes and made music to cook pasta to.

Much more up our particular avenue was Roy Wood. 'I believe that when you are performing you must provide a total show,' said Roy of Wizzard. This is a man who was known to change his hair colour every month and wear more face paint than a tribe of Sioux Indians. 'It must be something riveting and with the amazing make-up and hair it's pretty exciting,' he added needlessly. Musically, Wizzard dealt in a pastiche of Fifties rock 'n' roll. Actually, forget that. Everything that they did was a pastiche. Wizzard were another band who came up with the smart idea of a Christmas single. I Wish It Could Be Christmas Everyday.

Mott The Hoople? They weren't really Glam. They were just a bunch of old rockers Bowie took a shine to. He gave them his song, All The Young Dudes, and they got very big. But Glam? Nosiree, Bob. Alice Cooper? Again, he was something different. A theatrical rocker with a taste for the grand gesture, he was great. But in a different book. The Bay City Rollers? Get outta here. The Jackson Five? The New Seekers? Hot Chocolate? Abba? From Sweden, like Volvo? Puh-lease. Put your Post-modern irony away.

Then there were the sausage factory bands like White Plains and Paper Lace, Hudson-Ford and The New Seekers, bands who weren't really Glam at all but just got lumped in with the Sweets and the Muds because they happened to be knocking around the same neighbourhood at the same time. Chicory Tip. Do you remember Chicory Tip? Son Of My Father, that was their song. No one remembers Chicory Tip. I can't even remember them and I've just written about them. They were Glam by association. They'd be on the same edition of *TOTP*, but that was all. If anything, they got in the way.

Dancing Queens

There's one group we've missed out. One group who were omnipresent and pivotal, one group who were always there, who never missed a beat. One group who were always on *TOTP*. One group who always made a splash. Pan's People – Louise Clarke, Babs Lord, Dee Dee Wilde, Ruth Pearson, Cherry Gillespie, and choreographer Flick Colby. Every – and I mean every – schoolboy knew that line-up and could recite it like it was their football team. 'A handful of very dishy, very dolly dancing birds,' as they were described in 1974. To which I can only concur.

How many people do you think tuned in to *TOTP* just to watch Pan's People? Taking a ball park figure, I'd say about 40 per cent of the viewers. At the time, Pan's People were astonishingly sexy, astonishingly ravishing. It was, in the most literal of senses, a turn-on. There they were, every week, dancing their little socks off, giving, just giving.

To get a gauge of what it was like, put yourself back in 1972. There's *Top Of The Pops* – and nothing else. There's no *Chart Show*, no other TV show. There's no MTV, no VH-1, no anything. There are no pop videos. There's just *Top Of The Pops* and idiot groups miming along to their idiot hits. *Top Of The Pops* was incredibly powerful. Looking back, it's difficult to imagine quite how influential it was. The curious thing was, it was a crap old programme, patronisingly tedious and cheesy,

it talked to the 'kids' watching as if we were stupid.

Top Of The Pops was like the youth club where everyone went to see what was happening and the DJs were like trendy scoutmasters, old geezers who tried to pretend that they were one of us when we all knew that they would inform on us to our parents given half the chance. Even then, we knew that the DJs were a dreadful bunch, interested in only themselves, thinking they were the pop stars when really they were just cringingly embarrassing. Jimmy Saville, Tony Blackburn, Noel Edmonds, Ed 'Stewpot' Stewart, Kenny Everett, Peter Powell, Kid Jensen... Forget it. They were dreadful characters. So dreadful that they haven't been exhumed by the ravenous kitsch machine. So dreadful that there's nothing good that I can say about them at all. And you know what my mother always used to say? If you haven't got anything good to say about someone, don't say anything at all. The funny thing is, as the decade progressed, they got worse! Contemplate these three terrifying words: Dave Lee Travis. Sorry about that.

Dreadful as the DJs were, it didn't stop *TOTP* from being absolutely unmissable. Everyone watched it and if you didn't watch it... well, you just did. You couldn't not watch. Most of the time it was cringe-worthy and the DJs were cringe-worthy and your mum always walked in when there was something really stupid on and it would be really embarrassing, but what could you do? All the groups were on it – if you wanted to make a splash, *TOTP* was the place to go.

Bowie going down on Mick Ronson's guitar? That was TOTP. Roxy Music doing Virginia Plain? That was TOTP. Top Of The Pops was so influential you could make a grand gesture by not appearing on it. Led Zeppelin were one of the few groups to refuse to go on TOTP – which was funny, seeing as their most famous song, Whole Lotta Love (albeit the CCS version), was the show's theme tune from 1973 to 1981.

One of the few good things – maybe the only good thing – about *TOTP* was Pan's People. Pan's People were in the show where the pop videos would be now. There'd be a group who wouldn't come on, maybe they were Americans or on tour or too busy, so what were they going to do to illustrate the song? *TOTP* could play the song but what could they do about the visuals? Send for Pan. So Pan and her People would come on and do a dance. And they were incredibly sexy, incredibly... vibrant. Their little syncopated steps and that cute finger wagging to the camera thing that they

did. The flowing limbs and hair, the clothes wafting around their bodies, the skirts that were always, always split up the sides, the tassels that hung down over the exposed bits, cheekily giving a glimpse of the land beyond as they swivelled and swirled and danced and played. We used to sit there and try and guess what song they'd have Pan's People dance to. Mud? Nah, they'll be in the studio. Sweet. Nah, they'll also be there. And so you'd think of some American soulster who'd be too busy doing Soul Train in America which we knew was a brilliant show, but we never saw it. We once saw Bowie doing Young Americans on it and he was brilliant and it was brilliant. Top word, brilliant.

But Pan's People, you'd always want them to be dancing to a fast song, something that they'd do a lot of the old swivelling and swirling to, and by and large they would. Every so often they'd dance to some soft ballad and it would be sooooo disappointing, sooooo disappointing. They'd just waft around in these full-length chiffon things, trying to look all ethereal and sensual, but...listen, I don't know how to phrase this. Let's be bold. You never saw anything. There. Said it. We wanted hot pants and skirts with slits and tassels, not nonsense long chiffon things.

Pan's People. It's got to be said, there was an element of the underwear section in the mail order catalogue (if you know what I mean) to Pan's People. When I was a young lad, I used to send away for mail order catalogues (in my mother's name, stupid) and then I'd be really cool when they came, not say anything. Invariably, my mum would open them and have a look. She'd never buy anything, but she'd look. When she went, I'd go and sneak a look at the underwear section. Pre-teen soft porn. Well – and, listen, we're being honest here – there was an element of that in Pan's People. An element? Not 'arf.

Everyone had their favourite PP and they always did that looking at the camera – just at you – bit, and it was all a huge come-on. They each had

their own colour, their own moves. They each had their own tics, little things that they'd do, that the others wouldn't.

It's somewhat shocking now to talk to Ruth and Babs and hear them say things like… What am I talking about? It's somewhat shocking now to talk to Ruth and Babs? It's a bizarre fantasy to be sitting next to them, let alone talking to them. Maybe if I found myself talking to *Ziggy Stardust*-era Bowie it would be more of a nerve-jangling deal. No, thinking about it, even that doesn't compare. The only comparison would have to be sitting next to Marc Bolan – and only then that's because he's dead.

Pan's People – 'The name? We got the name from Pan, the goddess of dance,' said Ruth. 'Hahahahaha,' I said laughing like a hyena, like I was sitting next to Groucho Marx or something. 'Of course, hahaha.' Then I knocked the tea pot over. And then spilt the milk while trying to clean up the tea pot.

'It was electric and thrilling and I have wonderful warm memories,' said Dee Dee, always my sister's favourite. 'For a young girl it was the best job in the world. We were in the public eye, at the top of our profession and admired by millions.'

We all had a great time in the Sixties and Seventies. 'I can remember being in that small intimate studio with Stevie Wonder and it was magic. But it was also quite lonely as well at times. Men were keen to look but they wouldn't come near us. We were so glamorous they thought we were unapproachable. And men will never approach a group of women, especially a loud, attractive group of young women.'

Flick Colby, the only American in the gang, said, 'We were always much more than a dance team. We were a group, except that we didn't sing. We were just kinda like session musicians. We just got together because we all liked dancing. We just wanted to go out and start leaping around, so we did.

'As a dance group, Pan's People always had something to say, and that was always reflected in our dancing.' Er, yes. Know what you mean, Flick. Sweet Flick. Always a way with words. In 1974, she said this: 'The girls were all picked because they were good dancers, although good looking girls obviously help any group along. The more they dance, the more sexy they are to watch. But Pan's People have never been 'teasers'. We've never tried the alluring technique.'

'Course.

'Of course we were sexy,' said Ruth. 'Young girls are sexy.'

Kitsch is something that it's impossible to be at the time that you're doing it. You can only be kitsch in retrospect. Mostly that's absolutely true, but – and I don't know how they pulled this off – Pan's People managed to pull off the unique trick of being contemporarily kitsch. There was a naïve charm that was innocence. What were they? Twenty? And now Babs talks about her daughter's boyfriend asking her for a picture so that he can show his mates. 'My daughter's boyfriend wants a picture of her mum!?' And Ruth talks about being at a party and sitting next to Paul McCartney and who's that walking past? Why, it's Mick Jagger.

Pan's People were perfect. Gorgeous gals in a pre-silicon age, they could have been you.

So I said to Ruth what were they like, all those parties? What was it like, backstage at *Top Of The Pops*? Was it a laugh? And Ruth looked at me and she said, 'Was it a laugh? It was such a laugh I can't tell you.' So, go on, what happened? 'I'd tell you, but to be honest, I can remember going out to lots of parties, but I can't really remember the detail.' You had a good time then. 'Oh, yes. It was fun.'

Young Americans At The English Disco

Meanwhile...

And it spread to America, which was fair enough. They gave us hippie, it was about time we gave them something back and I can't think of anything that America needed more in the early Seventies. It was deep in the quagmire that was Vietnam. Martin Luther King had been shot dead. Robert Kennedy had been shot dead. The peace-loving hippies had turned into militant Yippies and had turned political protest into, how shall we say, a more confrontational tool. If there was any last embers of the hippie dream burning, Charles Manson had wiped them out. Easy Riders blown away. What could little old England give its big cousin to cheer it up? Hey, I know. How about a chubby failed pop star with a hairy chest, bouffant hair, wrapped in Bacofoil and who sang on a song that had no words.

America embraced it with its usual grace. 'Irony? Don't want none of that communist bull round here, boy.' America's not very good with irony and it's not surprising that, given the same ingredients, we came up with Gary Glitter and they came up with The New York Dolls. While Gaz punched the air and asked us if we wanted to be in his gang (his gang, his gang. Did we wanna be in his gang? Oh, yeah!), the Dolls were strung out and complaining of having a personality crisis. America, bless. Land of the free – of a sense of humour, that is.

There's something that happens when America gets involved in what is essentially an English idea and that **something always manifests itself in the same way: it gets bigger and it loses its self-deprecatory sense of irony.** The fun goes. The same thing happened with punk a few years later. Whereas we had The Sex Pistols, The Clash and The Damned, they came up with The Germs and The Tubes. Still, that's a different chapter in a different book.

It's more to do with the nature of 'adoption' than any crass national characteristic. Where the British Glam scene grew out of a ridiculous sense of 'Ooh, I wonder what that looks like?', the American scene merely aped

what was happening here. Glam wasn't indigenous to America, it was a series of looks and mannerisms that they imported. Then once it had been imported, they added to it.

But what they added, only they could add.

Glam followed a well-worn path, a path that had been walked down by everyone from Nero to Chaplin to Errol Flynn to… I don't know. You, maybe. In LA, the story had taken in the silent stars of the Twenties, the Hollywood aristocracy of the Forties and the hippies of the late Sixties. The ritual was familiar. Everyone wanted to be near the stars and this, combined with the usual schtick – too much money in the hands of the young and fêted – led to a questionable air of decadence and abuse.

The court of the crimson kings was a place named with verve, imagination, irony and wit. It was called The English Disco, and this is its story.

Like England, life had gotten dull. As the Sixties turned into the Seventies, things were at a low ebb. After the flower power burn-out of 1968 when everything fell apart, psychedelia peeked through the curtains, decided it had had enough and disappeared up its own fractal imagery. Who wanted to take acid and trip into the subconscious when all you were likely to find was Vietnam and death? Who wanted to strut about like peacocks when, any second Postman Pat could come along and call you up? Quite. Possibly more crippling to the 'peace and love' merchants was the Charles Manson episode. After all, the west coast rock community, especially the Beach Boys, had welcomed Manson in, going so far as to record one of his songs. And then look what he does! That's gratitude.

Musically, things weren't so much bad as worse. The music was dead and quite a few of the people who made that music were dead, too. After all those glorious flights of fancy, things suddenly went introspective. And it was an introspection that wore cowboy boots. Serious country rock in serious jeans with, if you were really lucky, a serious beard at the top end. Could there be anything worse?

The prevalent sound was that of people falling asleep – people like Jackson Browne, Linda Ronstadt, the Allman Brothers, The Byrds. At the end of the road... The Eagles. Take away the pristine cynicism of Steely Dan – music to be admired, not to shag to (unless of course you were into tantric sex) – and what was there to have a laugh about?

Imagine. You're a young kid and you're surrounded by these whinging, whining singer-songwriters with their cowboy boots and their denims and their mature songs that ask questions about life and death and why wheat grows in straight lines. Imagine that. You're going to look for something else already, aren't you?

And that's how The English Disco came into being.

In early 1972, Rodney Bingenheimer, a young hang-around who'd hung around LA and Sunset Boulevard since the mid-Sixties, decided that he'd had enough of the beards and went off to London in search of some fun. A record company acolyte, he'd known David Bowie and Rod Stewart and gravitated towards them. Before you could say 'What is that you're wearing?', Rodney was knee-deep in platform boots and glitter and became a fully-fledged Anglo.

Bowie, with whom he hung out more and more, suggested that he start a club in Hollywood and in October 1972, the E-Club opened. (And, no, it's not that kind of E we're talking about.) Reasonably enough, the first guest was David Bowie – dressed as Ziggy Stardust. The idea took off and within months the club revamped itself and re-launched as Rodney Bingenheimer's English Disco.

'Rodney knew British singles and bands that even I wasn't aware of,' Bowie said later in Barney Hoskyns' excellent history of LA's music culture, *Waiting For The Sun*. 'He single-handedly cut a path through the treacle of the Sixties, allowing all us *avants* to parade our sounds of tomorrow dressed in our clothes of derision.' Tapping in to the new sound, The English Disco embraced everything English – as long as it looked and sounded glitter. But things quickly changed. In England, it was all Boots No 7 and Tiger Feet. In America, it was cocaine and under-age groupies.

What do you want to know? There was a group called Backstage Pass. It was an all-girl group. You want to be more basic? OK. Groupies were the currency of the day – the younger they were, the more value they had.

The new 'stars' of the scene were the likes of the 13-year-old Joan Jett (later of Glam punksters The Runaways), Sable Starr and Lori Lightning. It's interesting how punk those names are: what goes around, comes around.

Astonished at how they were revered, The Brit groups came out to play but, predictably, the Americans looked at them, ate them and then spat them out. But the groups kept going over. What was in the shop was just too attractive a proposition. It was every boy's dream.

All those bands we knew from *Top Of The Pops* as being 'just a bit funny really' suddenly had a cachet. They were cool. It's a bizarre notion, but maybe it's true. Here now they're acceptable because they're kitsch. Kitsch? OK, I can live with that. But cool?

Just to pursue a brief tangent, it's curious but the kings of this particular scene were Led Zeppelin. 'When they came to town they thought they could get away with anything,' remembers groupie queen Pamela Des Barres. And, by all accounts, they could. Stories of Zeppelin excesses are legion and not really relevant here – suffice to say they lived in a different world – but it's just an interesting example of how things were over there.

Nightclubbing,

All this isn't to say that America didn't have its own Glam icons. Iggy Pop. There. Said it. The Igster was Glam king (queen?) and smeared his presence over the scene like a pot of runny honey. Iggy had been hanging around for a few years and his proto-punk band The Stooges were a long-established tradition.

At this juncture we should maybe explain something. Right now, Iggy – and remember, this man was born in 1947 – is known for his ridiculously muscular body, his flowing locks, clear eyes and strong teeth. He's a veritable health advert. And his music? Everyone loves his music, especially since his classic Lust For Life was used in the film *Trainspotting*. In the late 1990s, Iggy Pop is a folkloric hero, pop culture's genial uncle. If he were an actor, he'd get one of those Oscars that they give to people who survive. But back in 1972…

If he'd been a horse, they would have shot Iggy Pop. What was the point of keeping him alive? He wasn't going to survive, he wasn't going to last the course. Why waste the food on him?

'Why waste the food on him?' was a good question, except that one look at him and you knew that no one wasted the food on him anyway. It wasn't so much that he was skinny, it's that he was… What's twice skinny? Iggy was

We're Nightclubbing

wasted. He was a relic from an earlier age, another age that didn't really want him. He was only a Face because Bowie had taken him under his wing. And since Bowie was the arbiter of cool, Iggy was cool.

Iggy was like the scene's plaything. A walking experiment. How many drugs can a human being take and still stay alive? Hey, there's Iggy Pop. Let's ask him.

In May 1973, Iggy released the Bowie-produced *Raw Power*. On the cover (*opposite*), Iggy stands against his microphone stand, silver straw hair hanging. He's wearing no shirt and his trousers are these tight Bacofoil hipsters that hang low. It's a classic shot, perfectly in synch with the first song on the album, Search And Destroy. The world's forgotten boy.

But any thoughts of a normal style career… No. This is Iggy Pop we're talking about. The Ig was downbeat about *Raw Power* – he hated the sound mix – fell back into heroin, got off it and fell into even worse habits. What did Iggy know? He was a drug addict. *Raw Power* was and remains a classic. *Creem* magazine said it was 'the best album of the Seventies'.

To the scenesters at The English Disco, Ig was an oddity, but he wasn't considered cool because – bizarrely – he wasn't English. As *NME* journalist Nick Kent recalls in *Waiting*

For The Sun, 'He was very quickly regarded as a loser, mainly because he wasn't English. My most abiding memory is of him standing at the English Disco in his *Raw Power* clothes, stoned, looking at himself in the mirrored walls for hours on end. It was pretty sad.'

Increasingly desperate, on August 11, 1974, Iggy appeared in a play at the Disco entitled *Murder Of The Virgin*. A neo-Nazi piece of **** (fill in your own expletive), it was sold as the night that Iggy was going to kill himself. In the end, all he did (all he did!) was to take a large butcher's knife and attack his chest with it. Bleeding stupid. It typified the whole Disco scene. People playing about like they were in a real-life version of *The Night Porter*. Playing. Bowie's Rebel Rebel had become the key song, but no one was rebelling. What happened to Iggy? Well, he didn't die – he probably didn't care enough – he just ended up in the Neuro-Psychiatric Institute.

At the end of the year, there was another play at the English Disco. *The Death Of Glitter* was another self-indulgent, drug-fuelled frenzy in which a coffin was carried around to the raucous sound of the New York Dolls' Personality Crisis.

Ahhh, the New York Dolls. The New York Dolls were, well, from New York. They weren't, though, dolls. Spiritually, they came from the same shop as Iggy Pop, all low-life poise and substance abuse. What they shared was a love for showing off, a love for making a spectacle of themselves. Urban street kids on the make, the Dolls rode the burgeoning Glam scene, getting themselves the look to go with an attitude that was already there. It was transvestite trash and they became a living cartoon. Clothes became loud, shoes became high, hair became big. And, again like Pop, it was the glamour of decadence. There was make-up, but it was smudged.

The connection was through their manager, Leee Black Childers. He'd been hanging around various scenes since time began – first at Andy Warhol's Factory in the Sixties and later at the English Disco. There, he'd been working as a fixer for Bowie's management group, MainMan. It was Childers who'd given Iggy his marching orders after the *Murder Of The Virgin* fiasco.

At heart, the Dolls were a punk band, a loud, thrashy, trashy guitar punk band. Raucous and fun. Surfing the zeitgeist that was peaking in LA, they were seen as desperately vogueish and trendy and their record label Mercury threw money at them and employed another glitter-ball, Todd Rundgren, to produce their debut album. Rundgren was hot, having only just released the frenetic psychedelic Glam collision *A Wizard, A True Star*, and had the Midas touch. Knowing the Dolls' reputation, Mercury hoped that they'd be safe in Rundgren's hands. OK, so he had rainbow streaked hair and looked like a glitzy anorexic horse, but he was also a serious muso and would do the job. 'It was chaotic,' Rundgren's girlfriend, the infamous rock star appendage Bebe Buell said later. 'Being around the New York Dolls was like *Willie Wonka's Chocolate Factory*.' What did she mean?

Released in August 1973, *New York Dolls* sounded just as it should have. The song titles – Bad Girl, Pills, Trash, Frankenstein, Vietnamese Baby, Jet Boy, Personality Crisis, Looking For A Kiss – tell you all you need to know. 'They were the greatest fun you could imagine,' it was said later.

What became of the New York Dolls? The short answer is 'not as much as should have'.

Like Iggy, they were a band who played lead needle and rhythm guitar – and that's a combination that doesn't necessarily guarantee career prospects. Look, one of them (drummer, Billy Murcia) died in 1972. That should have given some warning. Lead singer David Johannsen looked like Mick Jagger in a dress, but guitarist Johnny Thunders drove the bus and he resembled Keith Richards as much in, how shall we say, hobbies as appearance.

In early 1975, they approached embryonic svengali Malcolm McLaren to look after them. A provocateur even in those days, McLaren dressed them up in red communist outfits and sent them out to shock an America still in love with the Cold War. America didn't really care and that, really, was the Dolls.

Thunders and drummer Jerry Nolan found a degree of fame in the late Seventies with Johnny Thunders' Heartbreakers, but their first hit was the drug anthem Chinese Rocks and it was obvious where their true love lay. In a sad but inevitable end to the story, Johnny Thunders died of a drugs-related cause on 23 April 1991.

There's another character to consider in the story of American Glam: Lou Reed. Reed had already altered the course of rock/pop once with The Velvet Underground, arguably the most influential group ever, but by the early Seventies he was a bit of a lost bunny. He'd left the Velvets in 1970 and a solo album apart (1972's *Lou Reed*, a curio where, bizarrely, Reed was backed up by Rick Wakeman and Steve Howe of prog rockers Yes) he wasn't up to much. Well, nothing much apart from – and you should be able to guess this by now – a singular devotion to destroying his health.

The similarities between Reed and Iggy didn't end there. Both were dragged out of their drug-induced creative slumber by the gentle hand of the arch-philanthropist David Bowie. It's a curious thing, Bowie's philanthropy. He kept taking these people under his wing – and there were other recipients during this time, most notably and most successfully Mott The Hoople – giving them strength and songs and sending them on their way. (Typically, they took his song *All The Young Dudes* and then split, figuring they didn't need him.) Yet he himself was as strung out and barely alive as they, generally, were.

'Lou has been a powerful influence on a host of contemporary performers… myself included,' said David Bowie. What more could anyone want?

Reed came to London to do a gig with Bowie at The Royal Festival Hall and threw his hat firmly in the ring by coming on with glitter and eye make-up.

Sweetly, the concert was a Save The Whales charity do. 'I did three or four shows like that, then it was back to leather. We were just kidding around – I'm not into make-up,' said Lou, careful not to scratch his black nail varnish.

Whatever, under the watchful eye of producer Bowie and helped by guitarist Mick Ronson, Reed came back with the triumphal *Transformer*, an album soaked in decadent imagery, stiletto style. Initially known as much for its cover – and especially the back cover – as the music, *Transformer* broke Reed through to a whole new audience. Each song was a classic dealing in one depravity or another. 'There's a lot of sexual ambiguity on the album,' said Reed, but the stand-out, the one that captured the imagination was the single A Walk On The Wild Side, a tale of the good times back at Andy Warhol's Factory, the Velvet Underground's alma mater, and a song that gained credibility by sneaking through the radio censors despite having a lyric that contained the phrase 'giving head'. It's always a treat when we get one past the authorities and that's what A Walk On The Wild Side did. 'Any song that mentions oral sex, male prostitution, methedrine, valium and still gets Radio 1 airplay must be truly cool,' said Nick Kent.

The BBC, bless, never did admit to their error, and it's a sweet irony that 25 years later the BBC used to flip side of Wild Side, Perfect Day, as the soundtrack to their first self-advertising commercial.

Which only leaves Leon Russell, a New Orleans pianist who brought the musicianship and drugs to Joe Cocker's infamous *Mad Dogs And Englishman* tour in 1970, and whose debut LP carries a back cover photo strangely reminiscent of T.Rex's *Slider* (the pic of Bolan on which was taken by Ringo Starr, who happened to be a pal of Mr Russell…). The album also contained a song titled Roll Away The Stone which could be, but isn't the same song as recorded by Mott The Hoople five years later. Weird, huh? Anyway, that basically was American Glam. It was as far from the British idea as you could imagine. It was a small, self-important coterie, who never looked – and never wanted to look – outside their own front-door. NY Glam was a sex-obsessed little monkey strung out on cocaine, Californian Glam came to be characterised as ego. In England, it was all 'laugh at me'. In America, it was 'look at me'.

Back of original album cover

It's a curious thing. Away from the world of music, America was as jolly and light and fluffy as anything we threw up. The telly that came from the States – best exemplified by the likes of *Charlie's Angels* and *The Six Million Dollar Man* – was top Glam. But music is the core of any cultural movement and American music…

For an idea of how American Glam differed from British Glam, consider pop Glamsters The Sweet. When they were over here, The Sweet made records called things like Little Willy and Wig-Wam Bam. The record they made there they called Desolation Boulevard. Sex and drugs and rock 'n' roll. Never was it more true than in the American – specifically, the LA – Glam scene of the early Seventies.

The irony in all of that is that the music that came out of the American scene was light years ahead of its British equivalent – Bowie excepted. What this tells us about drugs…doesn't bear thinking about.

Kings and Queens of Television

It's no coincidence that **Britain** embraced Glam at precisely the moment that colour television sets became affordable. It was a visual revolution which would see metaphorical blood shed, and a new order arise. Out went any series which looked great in black and white but lacked the imagination to capitalise on the potential of colour images. *Andy Pandy*, *Lamb Chop* and *Bill And Ben* stood no chance against the Glam appeal of *Crystal Tips And Alistair*, *The Wombles* (pop stars, even!) and *White Horses*. Any series which had previously been set-bound had to find its way out onto the streets to fully exploit the technicolour splendour of the new telly.

Being relatively new and thus brave and brash, ITV had the Glammest of Glam TV shows. The BBC might have had the writing talent (*Play For Today*, *Steptoe & Son*, *Til Death Us Do Part*, *Whatever Happened To The Likely Lads*), but the commercial channel had the fish 'n' chips eating, Woodbine-smoking, narrow ambitions of the Great British public in their writers minds. ITV knew how to work the glitz, captured the ready-rubbed seaside humour which was just beginning to work its package-flight way to the Costa del Sol. The BBC had history, but ITV had the day. The world was changing, and ITV was determined not just to watch it change, but it wanted to be a part of that change. *On The Buses* undoubtedly had the sharpest, smartest producer in independent television.

Spy series had it made: airports, hotels, palm trees, casinos, electronic gadgetry were all crammed into such early outposts of Glam TV as *The Saint*, *The Baron*, *Man In A Suitcase*, *Crane*, *The Avengers*. The heroes, who would

Right: International Man of Mystery, Cravat and Handlebar Moustache – Jason King

operate in a different international location for each episode, were all suitably ambiguously employed. *The Baron* was a jet age antique dealer who owned exclusive shops in London, Paris and Washington and also worked as an undercover agent for the police and government. Roger Moore's Brylcreemed Simon Templar in *The Saint*, who was a kind of freelance instrument of justice, easily made the transition to colour via various international ports, while the lesser-known *Crane* was a Moroccan-based smuggler who owned a rundown cafe in Casablanca. *The Avengers*, which had made a name for itself in the Sixties by employing surreal black and white images in dazzling arrays of technical wizardry, sexy female leads in black leather and white Lotus Elans and the odd (indeed) car chase, had run its course by the early Seventies. It did return at the end of Glam with the wrong exotic location (Canada) and wrong car – Purdey's rust-prone Triumph TR7 – but with a kitsch appeal all of its own.

The fact is, of course, that it didn't matter what the heroes and heroines of the Glam shows actually did or how they were paid, as long as they were living lives beyond the norm. With the coming of colour, the life was there to be witnessed and copied: *Department S*, *The Protectors*, *The Prisoner*, *The Champions*, *The Persuaders*, all offered views to a Glam new world.

The ultimate in Glam heroes left the successful Sixties spy series *Department S* in 1971. Jason King, gloriously played by the Figaro-moustached Peter Wyngarde, was a ludicrous rake who operated as a most unlikely

international best-selling author-come-counter-espionage agent. Of course, this was entirely a front for his true occupation: that of a bizarrely-besuited Glam clothes horse. King/Wyngarde was arguably the only character in television history (in human history!), born to wear spearpoint-collared shirts, bulbously knotted ties and pin-striped suits that flared into absurdity. Although, sadly, Jason King clones were rarely spotted walking down the local High Street, they did appear as photographic models in every Unisex hairdressers in the land; as pencil drawings on small advertisements for brushed denim flares which appeared in the rear end of the tabloids; and as the gravel-voiced hero in no small number of soft porn movies. (Curiously, Jason King also seems to appear on a million Seventies wedding photographs. He is usually some distant uncle or friend of a friend who was never heard of again.)

Above: Reg Varney chases the wimmin in *On the Buses*.
Below: Richard O'Sullivan chases the wimmin, Sally Thomsett and Paula Wilcox, in *Man About the House*

One of the most natural resting homes for Glam would be the British sitcom. Ever a patchy genre, it spent a good deal of the Sixties directly opposing the notion of Glam or glamour. There was no trace, for instance, in *Steptoe And Son* (unless you count the fact that Elton John chose Hercules as his middle moniker because it was the name of the *Steptoe*'s horse). But with the advent of colour, *On The Buses* and *Love Thy Neighbour* offered a brash streetwise Glam, while Clement and La Frenais' *Whatever Happened To The Likely Lads?*

perfectly encapsulated the everyday tension abroad in a Britain not long over rationing, where town centres still offered views into Second World War bomb craters and the unions held sway over the Government. Terry and Bob were the two faces of a country enjoying boom (Glam) and recession (glum) in quick succession. Terry was old Labour, old Britain, content with a few pints, birds and football, an eternal Lad; Bob was the flared-lapelled, fat tie-wearing social climber moving into his first, newly-built home with wife and new Vauxhall Viva.

On the opposite coast of England, beginning in 1969, Carla Lane's garishly clad *Liver Birds* had started to hint at a new-found feminist freedom. Created as something of a distaff *The Likely Lads*, the two girls, Beryl and Dawn, raged through a late Sixties Liverpool, embarrassing the male population with torrents of striking sexual innuendo.

Sex was a major ingredient in Glam. It was as if Britain had suddenly discovered sexual innuendo and was determined to see how far it could go. All the way, was the naturally smutty answer. Sex was a recurring theme of Glam sit-comedy and it was never more nakedly apparent than in the mighty *Man About The House* (1973-76), in which Chrissy (Paula Wilcox) and Jo (Sally Thomsett) were forced to share an Earls Court flat with the man that many considered to be the luckiest person alive, catering student Robin Tripp (Richard O'Sullivan). The situation, in which the two girls had to initially conceal Tripp's presence from snooping landlord George Roper, was merely the backdrop for light-hearted sexual banter which, by later standards, seems astonishingly blatant. Strangely, despite the obvious glamour of the girls, it was Robin who made the most lasting impression. Heavily sideburned and strikingly garbed in denim coats, roller penny-collared shirts with patchwork patterns, Oxford bags and platform shoes, Robin Tripp was the perfect example of street level Glam. *Man About The House* produced two spin-offs, both of which contained hints of Glam. In *Robin's Nest*, Tripp had set up a restaurant with his live in girlfriend, Vicky (Tessa Wyatt, the ex-Mrs Tony Blackburn), which continued the trendy domestic situation while George Roper and his wife moved to leafier areas to chastise each other in *George And Mildred* – played by Yootha Joyce, who was quite the epitome of pink lampshade 'n' frills suburban Glam.

3 CLASSIC EPISODES FROM ONE OF TV'S ALL-TIME FAVOURITE COMEDIES

George & Mildred

JUMBLE PIE
ALL AROUND THE CLOCK
THE UNKINDEST CUT OF ALL

PG

Well 'ard, darlin'!

The problem with hippies was that they were all a bit soft. All of that putting flowers in rifle barrels wasn't going to stop people getting hurt, was it? Glam might have looked on the surface as if it was a lot of blokes poncing about on high heels in make-up but look a little closer and you'll more often than not see that it isn't eye makeup, it's a black eye. Men wanted to look Glam but remain masculine – hard. *The Sweeney* offered two perfect male role models in the shape of Jack Regan (John Thaw) and George Carter (Dennis Waterman). An eternally celebrated self-parodying blast of screaming tyres and blasting shotguns, *The Sweeney* started life as an *Armchair Theatre* entry, *Regan*, in 1974. For the next four years no other series so successfully captured the inelegance of mid-Seventies man, filled as it was with vast triangular jacket collars, tie knots like beer barrels and criminals garbed in ill-fitting bomber jackets, all trying their hardest

to look like Jason King if he shopped at C&A. The fact that each episode would have at least one car chase involving those Glam chariots the Ford Granada and Morris Marina just added to the Glam appeal.

Where Regan and Carter led, others followed. *The Professionals* down-scaled *The Sweeney*'s element of menace into genuine farce in a futile attempt to put a high gloss on their Glam. The two lead characters were ex-SAS hard cases Bodie and Doyle (Lewis Collins and Martin Shaw) whose rugby club, bitter-drinking machismo attempted rather more refinement than Regan and Carter. This was, by comparison, sophisto-Glam. These two, while hardly being 'new men' – which wouldn't be Glam at all – knew a thing or two about good wines, gourmet food and, one always presumed, exotic sex. Regan and Carter, on the other hand, preferred beans on toast, two cans of lager and a quickie with some long-suffering, mistreated wife of an old lag who had been put away by our unholy heroes. Bodie and Doyle had more Glam cars: a Ford Capri Mk II 3.0, a 3.5 Rover P6 and Range Rover, but if it had ever come to a punch-up between the casts of the two shows, the smart money was always on Jack and George.

Both *The Sweeney* and *Professionals* were British versions of what was, essentially, an American genre: the cop show. Since they had been making TV series for longer than the Brits, the Americans had the edge in terms of sheer numbers. By the early 1970s there was a whole slew of American cop shows on telly in the UK. Some were too worthy to watch – *Ironside* (dull and grey, featured a man in a wheelchair), *Cannon* (some car chases, but come on, a fat man?!?). But some were too groovy not to watch – *Kojak* featured the brilliant, weird-looking, lollipop-sucking baldy Telly Savalas (and his fat brother), had lots of car chases shot on the streets of exotic and frightening New York, and normally involved a shooting or two. *Starsky And Hutch* was the American version of *The Professionals* (or rather, vice-versa), and was unmissable not for the asinine plots, but the ridiculous clothes worn by the lead characters (played by Paul Michael Glaser and David Soul). *Starsky And Hutch* was also unmissable for those Glam fans hip enough to recognise in one Huggy Bear the presence of a very real street-style icon. Huggy was the epitome of street chic with his floor-length leather coat, tam-o'-shanter knitted hat, huge platforms and flared white suit. Like the Chi-Lites, Fatback Band, Barry White, Ohio Players, Marvin Gaye and Curtis Mayfield, Huggy Bear looked cool in clothes that made the average Brit Glam fashion victim look exactly what he was: a building labourer done up like an extra from a cheap skin-flick.

Glam wasn't all about men looking like big girls' blouses, though. There were plenty of female Glam role models, too. Well, to be exact there were three and naturally they were American: *Charlie's Angels*, were all gorgeous women

Below: Crimefighters *Starsky and Hutch*. The cardie did it.

who, for some vague reason, were working for an unseen authority (Charlie), to solve various crimes and mysteries. None of which mattered a jot, as the whole point of the show was to showcase the trio of awesome girls, who all lived together, shopped together and were forever striking alarming *Vogue*-ish poses with guns in hand. It was Glam because it simply had no pretensions whatsoever except to look good, and provided the world with its first glimpse of Farrah Fawcett (she was later to add Majors to her name when she married Lee, the world's first bionic man, star of *The Six Million Dollar Man*). Once known as an *Angel*, Farrah's remarkable hair, teeth and legs would adorn more bedroom walls than any other poster icon in the world, ever, and flash a smile on a million bottles of shampoo, hair -dye and bubble-bath. Her co-stars Kate Jackson, Cheryl Ladd and, as Farrah's replacement, Cherry Tiegs, would go on to long and glorious careers in a thousand made-for-TV movies. At the time *Charlie's Angels* made a significant contribution to British fashion by boosting sales of glittery boob-tubes and bright blue eye liner.

Strike a pose – *Charlie's Angels:* **the baddies gave into them only too willingly**

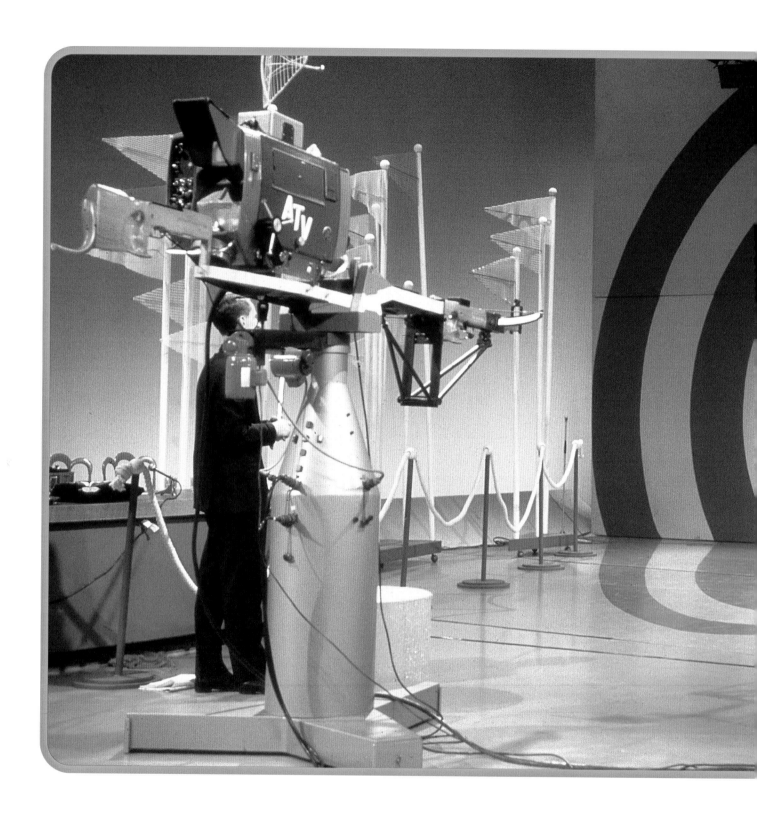

Bernie, The Bolt

ameshows are arguably the perfect televisual home for Glam. Most offered little more than a set wrapped in silver foil, a cheesy host, an endless parade of hapless contestants and a vague theme or concept. One thinks immediately of *The Golden Shot* (1967-75), most famously hosted by Bob Monkhouse with the assistance of The Golden Girls – Carol Dilworth, Andrea Lloyd and Anita Richardson initially, all easily out-glammed by regular helper Anne Aston, who had a maths A-level. The contestants, selected both from home viewers and the studio audience, had to guide a blindfolded cameraman on a studio 'tele-bow' and instruct him when to fire on various picture targets. Although supposedly a triumph of form and technology, the best bits, inevitably, came when the tele-bow failed to work, throwing Monkhouse into a diverting tirade of one-liners. For a while it was an essential part of Sunday afternoon although the show would weaken as later hosts, Charlie Williams and Norman Vaughan, would struggle to maintain Monkhouse's degree of unadulterated smarm.

You Can't Fool The Children Of The Revolution

Children's television in the Seventies was an inglorious mess of the mad, the daft and, mostly, the hugely patronising. It was a world inhabited by profoundly uncharismatic presenters wearing appalling jumpers and disturbing, cheesy grins. Even more alarming was their bizarre assumption that the nation's children would be eternally enthralled by the site of these sexless oiks creating something utterly pointless out of 'sticky back plastic' and used washing-up liquid bottles.

Apart from occasional shows by the Bay City Rollers, Flintlock and Arrows – artless, puerile but curiously entertaining and in the context of this book, absolutely non-essential shows – Seventies children's television was quite the antithesis of Glam.

And then came *Tiswas*. Created to challenge the staid, rigid format of the BBC's *Multi-Coloured Swap Shop*, Tiswas was loose, utterly shambolic,

deliciously subversive and was forever perched on the brink of chaos. Its leading male presenter, Chris Tarrant, looked for all the world as if he had all been on the beer the night before while his female counterpart, the eternally bedenimed and thigh booted Sally James, brought a breezy sexiness to Saturday morning television that, after years spent watching John Craven and Lesley Judd, seemed astonishingly provocative. Almost immediately, it

**Opposite: This Pic Ain't Big Enough For The Three Of Us –
Sally James, *Tiswas* presenter, gets plugged into Sparks,
below, has a heart-to-heart with Marc Bolan, and, right,
preparing for the Panto Years, a provocative puss-in-boots**

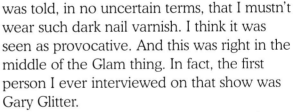

attained cult status, with *Tiswas* appreciation societies bursting into life in pubs and universities across the country.

Running from Glam to New Romantic, *Tiswas* sandwiched the punk years and will remain forever associated with the flamboyant fringes of pop style. Here, Sally James emerges from her latter-day retreat in deepest Surrey to guide us through the varying styles of the *Tiswas* years… and lots of other things.

'I began as an actress, in the Sixties. I was in *To Sir With Love* and did a few soap operas, things like that. I never thought about presenting television programmes at all until the idea for a London Weekend show, called *Saturday Scene*, came along. This was a young, pop magazine-type thing that spread across Saturday mornings. Frankly, they wanted a denim-clad bird to front it…and I was that bird. Just to indicate how strange attitudes were at the time, I was hauled in for an audition and was told, in no uncertain terms, that I mustn't wear such dark nail varnish. I think it was seen as provocative. And this was right in the middle of the Glam thing. In fact, the first person I ever interviewed on that show was Gary Glitter.

'*Tiswas* had already started in Birmingham and there was a rumour going around that it would be networked and so they had started to look for a girl to sit alongside Chris Tarrant. Chris was initially against this. He thought it was a lads' show, really. Not the kind of thing that some girlie should get involved in. Thinking about it now, I can understand what he meant. But it certainly didn't soften when it was networked and I came in. Not a bit of it.'

Noddy Holder

'Yes, we spent a lot of time sitting round, watching television. Television was great at the time. I loved the lads' shows, the cop shows. Like *The Sweeney*. That whole Ford culture, Transit vans skidding all over the place and all that tough talk. It seemed really natural at the time but when you see them today it's all really forced. Hilarious. But we were lads and it was a lads' show. Loved it. What else? *Department S*, *The Professionals*, *Budgie*. That was daft, wasn't it? I'd love to see it now. It was different back then because there wasn't as much TV, so everyone seemed to be watching the same show. Whenever we appeared on TV, the next day, everyone would be saying, "Didn't like that outfit Dave was wearing", or whatever. That kind of helped push the thing along. We were televisual. Very televisual.'

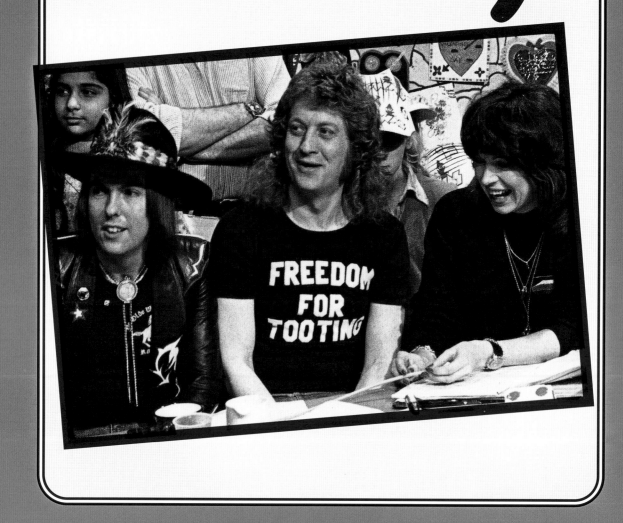

Get It On!

I think I must have been about 13. Maybe 14. I remember I persuaded my mother that I needed a new pair of shoes and – and looking back, I've no idea how I did this – persuaded her to give me the money to buy them. 'Listen, there's a shoe shop near school. I'll nip out during the lunch break and get a pair'. I don't know. Does that sound plausible? Doesn't to me. But it happened. As soon as she gave me the money – £20 I think – I knew what I was going to do. I'd done my research, you see. I went to a shop called Shellys in Holloway, north London, and ... and... it was like walking into an Aladdin's Cave. There were more platforms than there were at Kings Cross station and they were splendid things. Like birds of paradise, they were shiny, metallic, glittery, colourful. I had to have a pair. How'd I explain it? That was tomorrow's problem and tomorrow never comes. I knew that because my mother had banged it into my head ever since I'd started school. 'You can't put off your homework until tomorrow, Jeremy.' She'd say. 'Tomorrow never comes.'

After about 15 seconds deliberation, I found myself trying on a pair of boots that were to die for. They had what was called a 'sandwich' sole – different layers on top of each other. I had metallic blue and silver, three layers. Blue, silver, blue. The heel was five inches high. The colour of the boot was the metallic blue, and at the front there was a silver flame going up to the top. They were like a palace for your feet. OK, I couldn't walk in them, but who needed to walk?

That night at the dinner table, there was only one subject of conversation. Listen, war could have been declared and there would have only been one subject of conversation...

'Jeremy, did you buy a pair of shoes for school? Bring them in, let's have a look at what meshiga shoes you've got.'

What happened next, I can't exactly recall. It's like you're looking through a photo album and there's a snap missing. She probably said something, maybe 'Mmmm, they're nice. Do you think they sell them in my size?' I can't remember.

That night at the dinner table, there was only one subject of conversation. Listen, war could have been declared and there would have only been one subject of conversation. My sister could have announced she was gay and there would have only been one subject of conversation. Mind you, if she'd have said that she was gay and her girlfriend wasn't Jewish...

We sat there, the whole meal, me, my sister, my mother, my father and, sitting there, like a fifth person, like a friend we'd invited round, my boots.

My father, bless, was a bit of a comic and this was like manna from the Gods for him. While my mother tutted and sighed and wondered what the neighbours would say – 'Going out dressed like that! And if somebody sees you... What am I going to say?' – and my sister talked about how stupid I was (this was a girl who only a few years earlier had been walking around with cow-bells around her neck), my father gagged around, addressing questions to my boots, talking to them as though they were, well, there. Me, I died.

They were perfect, my boots. I wore them in my bedroom every day. There was only one problem with my boots. I didn't have the right trousers to wear them with. I had trousers, of course, but not the right trousers. 'Mum...'

The next Friday there was a disco at this club in West Hampstead. Loads of people I knew were going. I was going to go. And I was going to show them what was what. Now then. Going out on Friday nights was a bit of a ritual. Home from school, straight upstairs to my room to sort out what I was going to wear. Supper was early because dad came home early on Fridays because it was the weekend. So, I do the supper thing, then back upstairs to change and... out.

Getting ready. I loved getting ready. Trying on this, seeing what that looked like. What do you think? That top with those trousers? Someone's parent would scoop us all up and give us a lift to wherever it was we were going or, more likely, the nearest tube station. This week – natch – it was my old man's turn. If it had been someone else's dad I could have flown down the stairs, shouted through to them in the lounge 'OK, I'm off now. See you later' and be gone. But no. This week, oh joy, it was my old man's turn.

'Come on then. Let's see what schmutters you're wearing.'

'He's got new trousers, Lou. I can't tell you.'

'New trousers. What are they? Metallic blue?'

The trousers, I've got to tell you, were perfect. High-waisted Oxfords, they were tight where it mattered and then, just below the bum, they flared out into this mass of flared bagginess. Halfway down the right thigh there was a stitched-on pocket. They were perfectly long – they reached the ground, but didn't drag along it. All that was fine and good, but nothing more than you'd ask from any pair of trousers. These though, these were perfect. They were so flared that they completely covered my priceless boots. When I walked in them, all you could see was this flash, this flash of something very, very flash. At the top, there was a waistband to kill for. High enough for five vertical buttons, they stopped halfway between my navel and my nipples. Above the waistband, I had a tank top. It was like a horizontal rainbow on top of which was an elaborately embroidered aeroplane. A shirt with a proper elephant collar completed the outfit.

I took a look in my mirror before going downstairs, trying to work out what they would take the piss out of but, really, what could they say?

'I can't see the boots. What's the point of the boots? You buy these boots and then you buy trousers that cover up the boots. If you didn't buy the boots you wouldn't have to have such wide trousers. Did you think of that?'

What were they? Stupid?

Supertroopers Abba
might well have proven
to be denim's Waterloo

Borne Up To Heaven On A Sea Of Denim

What other decade would be known both as the "Me" decade and The Decade That Taste Forgot. If for no other reason, that's good enough reason to love the Seventies. It's a curious thing. Taken one at a time, those two descriptions are perfect. Put them together and...Me, taste, forgot? No, no. That's someone else's taste that was forgotten, surely.

'It must have been about 1973 and I bought a pair of fantastic black boots with four inch heels and a wedge that was as thick as a hardback edition of The Complete Works of Shakespeare. I wore them with baggy black trousers and a skinny black top. Do you want to know about my

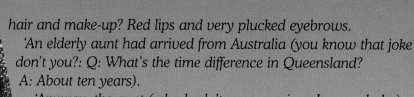

hair and make-up? Red lips and very plucked eyebrows.
'An elderly aunt had arrived from Australia (you know that joke
don't you?: Q: What's the time difference in Queensland?
A: About ten years).
'Anyway, the aunt (who hadn't seen me since I was a baby)
was helping my mother with the washing-up and suddenly said
in a very quiet and concerned voice: "I didn't know that
Jennifer had to wear orthopaedic shoes. Is it a club foot that she has?"
What could you say?'   **Jennifer Selway**

One of the best things about Glam fashion was that it was always available, and never over-priced. It had the effect of making its superstars somehow seem more human, more approachable. The Americans would claim it to be a proof of their Dream working. The Brits would never be so silly.

One of the most universally desired sex-symbols of Glam was Sally James, star of probably the greatest Glam kids' television show ever, *Tiswas*. She is our guide to the dress habits of the great, good and cor-blimey of Glam:

'There was a great irony about *Tiswas*...it always had this Glam image, mainly because all the Glam artists came onto the show. But the funny thing was that, because most of them knew full well that they would get soaked in water, they often tended to dress down a bit. We'd get Sweet on, for instance, and they would have reverted to denim, probably because they didn't want us to ruin their clothes. I didn't blame them. We ruined a lot of clothes on *Tiswas*. Glammed up pop stars don't look so charismatic when they are dripping in water or covered in slime. But I think most of them came on because it was refreshing for them. It was loose. They could hang about, have a laugh. I know that all the Glam bands were very competitive in the way they dressed. So *Tiswas* was a good antidote to all that. They had to be up for it. Also, it was a good way for the public to see a little beyond the image, because their was no way they could seem distant and charismatic. Image wise, they were naked.

'For my part, the Glam thing was casual anyway. I'd wear tight denim jeans, a little waistcoat and, of course, the thigh-length black leather boots. They were almost like waders really. They don't seem a bit stylish now but I really loved them at the time. They became a bit of a problem...I'd get a lot of quite

**Above: Jean Genies, the family Bowie – Angie, little Zowie and
David – definitely not the C&A types**

pervy letters flooding in. I don't think I was allowed to see the worst of them either. I think I was shielded from that, but some of them were pretty bad. The boots were undeniably a Glam item. I had one pair that I particularly liked. They came up to mid-thigh and had diamante all down the sides and really high spiked heels. I thought they were the bee's knees but I couldn't walk in them nowadays. I would wear them at night. Like a lot of people, dressing in Glam clothes meant party clothes. They weren't fashionable. Fashionable clothes were things like Oxford bag trousers and Budgie coats. But Glam meant 'fun' clothes. Things that you could wear for parties but would never wear walking down the street. I had

> **One of the things about the Glam era was that the girls always wanted to dress like men. It wasn't particularly feminine, which is kind of ironic when you think about it.**

a lot of those. I would go down to a shop called Ace on the Kings Road, where they would sell all this incredible stuff. Sequins everywhere. Lurex cardigans. I loved satin and velvet. I remember one outfit, dark blue satin trousers and a silver satin jacket. I thought that was really cool. My wardrobe was full of dark velvet flares, too. One of the things about the Glam era was that the girls always wanted to dress like men. It wasn't particularly feminine, which is kind of ironic when you think about it. Throughout that entire era I never owned a single skirt. Yeah, women went for a man-like look. Women liked to wear black while the men experimented with colour...so it was crossdressing in a really light fun kind of way. One favourite was outsize men's suits, like pin-striped gangster suits with massive ties. Or those silk jackets with the huge tulip collars, light green or metallic blue.

'In reality, *Tiswas* was anti-Glam. I'd dress down and just look at presenters. Bob Carol-Gees and Chris Tarrant – the scruffiest men on television. It makes

Below: Mud. They may have had Tiger Feet, but everything else came in denim

me laugh when things like this book cast Chris in a Glam image. I think he wore that same patched leather jacket throughout the entire run of *Tiswas*. There was one particular interview where, for some reason, he had to look smart. So he sent his shoes down to make up to be cleaned. Someone picked them up and instantly threw them in the bin. Chris went mad, he was shouting, 'They are my best shoes...what have you done with them?' But the girls down there just thought they were so disgusting that no one would want to wear them. It was seen as quite anarchic...to be so scruffy on television in those days. But it made people relax. It gave the thing a casual air.'

Keep On

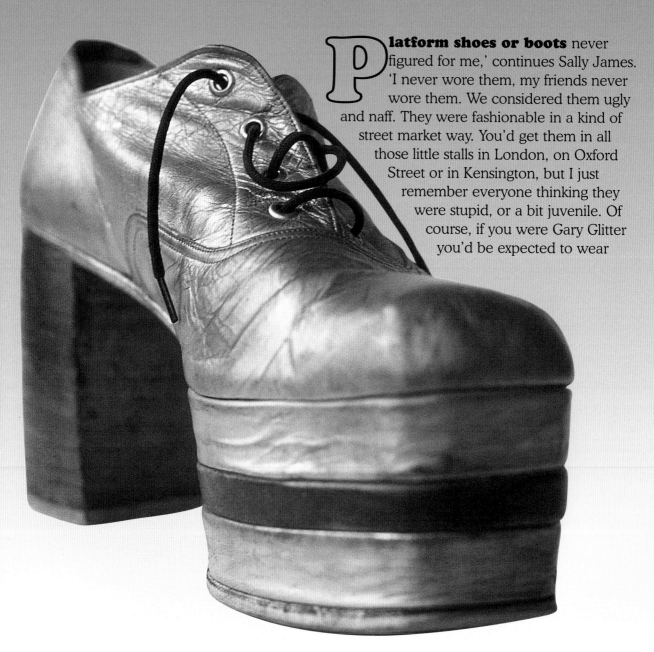

Platform shoes or boots never figured for me,' continues Sally James. 'I never wore them, my friends never wore them. We considered them ugly and naff. They were fashionable in a kind of street market way. You'd get them in all those little stalls in London, on Oxford Street or in Kensington, but I just remember everyone thinking they were stupid, or a bit juvenile. Of course, if you were Gary Glitter you'd be expected to wear

Truckin'

them. I remember talking to him in the dressing room and he seemed quite small and then, ten minutes later, he'd come staggering out onto the set, it seemed as if was about a foot taller. Ridiculous for *Tiswas* because people were always getting pushed over, but Gary was Gary, all decked out in that silver stuff. Nobody ever wore that on the street. People tended to pick up on bits of things from pop stars and used them in a rather more reserved way. Like Alvin Stardust would come on and would be wearing masses of rings. And then we'd be wearing lots of rings too, or lots of heavy fun jewellery around the neck. Things like that, cheap stuff. Anything would do. Things to catch the eye.

'I've just realised...I almost had platforms...or I, mean, had shoes that were almost platforms. They weren't real platforms, they were white wedges with a sandal top.

Ghastly shoes, absolutely ghastly. That was the thing about a lot of that Glam stuff, it was great fun but it never seemed like bad taste at the time. We really thought those things were stylish, back then. Absurd things seemed natural.

'A lot of them have been back in fashion since, but never quite the same. I love to look at wedding albums from the era. Now they are really embarrassing, especially for the lads, with long feathery hair, huge lapels and gigantic ties. Very funny now.'

Shang-a-Lang

There was the Tartan thing too. That didn't just belong to Bay City Rollers fans,' adds James. 'Tartan scarves were worn by a lot of older people, probably because of Rod Stewart. People in denim and tartan everywhere. I keep coming back to denim, not because that was my particular look, but because throughout the Glam period, denim was simply everywhere. People often forget that. You could 'Glam' denim up a bit. One big thing was sewing patches on, or embroidery. There was a lot of that. I had one pair of jeans with a few daft badges on, parrots and things, and I wore them for years and years, loved them. People would put studs in denim too. Not just rocker type studs, all kinds of studs. Heart shaped studs, strawberry-shaped studs, everything. There were those bizarre patchwork denim jeans, made up from all kinds of old Levi's, and cheaper denim too...and they would sell for immense amounts in London. They looked incredibly scruffy too, like old tramps trousers and people would wear them with white clogs...white clogs with thick wooden soles that fell off if you walked too fast. And little tiny patchwork denim waistcoats, Wrangler denim shirts. The whole ensemble. If it was winter you could even wear denim Budgie coats over the top of all this. Budgie coats with thick fluffy white collars. I didn't have one of those, they were more of a man's things I suppose, but I liked them.

Below: Rick Parfitt, centre, with *Tiswas'* Chris Tarrant, right. Parfitt only wore denim then. Come to think of it, he still does, Sally James is bottom left

'Status Quo were the Gods of denim. They always seemed to be on *Tiswas*. I'm sure that Rick Parfitt would just turn up and walk on, he was always there. I think that look was part of Glam, too... that whole thing about keeping your fags in the pocket of your Levi's jacket. Fags in one side, lighter in the other. Or in the pockets of cheese-cloth shirts. I had a few of those, they were cheap and very sexy.

'That's a look in itself. Sitting around the dressing room with Status Quo, drinking bloody Liebfraumilch, which was always flowing. Everyone felt it was really sophisticated at the time. It was just red, white or rosé in those days, wasn't it? Mateus Rosé. Disgusting stuff but you didn't now any different in those days. And Leibfraumilch kind of suited Status Quo's image, I think. Unpretentious...the wine of the people!

Born To Boogie

'Mike [Smith, Sally's husband] and I became very friendly with Marc Bolan in the later years. He was the epitome of Glam...absolutely. No one else came close. He looked so beautiful, all the time. I did quite a bit of modelling with him and it was always great fun. That possibly summed the era up, in a way, because here was Marc, all dolled up like a peacock...literally, with and everything and I'd be stood in plain denim. Like role reversal in a way. He used to wear tons, and I mean tons, of make up. Took him hours to get it all on. It was an artform for him. But he was a really, really nice man. Of course he was gregarious, he played that star role to the full and, no doubt, he really loved himself, but underneath all that he was actually a really nice, caring, intelligent guy. We'd have many dinner parties with him and he'd always be theorising on great heavy subjects, pontificating on this and that. Yes, he always had a lot to say, and maybe it was part of his showing off. But that was the whole point of Marc, wasn't it? That was the point of Glam. To show off.

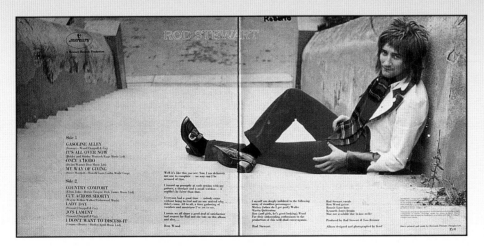

Left: Fashion statement or patriotic fervour? Rod Stewart wears tartan as only he can. Thankfully

Right: The Hairy Cornflake, Radio 1 DJ Dave Lee Travis, passes judgement on Glam's Miss Beautiful Eyes contest. Never mind the hot-pants

Marc was it...perfect, always absolutely perfect. Actually those tulip satin jackets were very Marc, weren't they? Only thing is, he wore a pink feather boa as well.

'It's difficult to compartmentalise that era. It wasn't just a question of, all of a sudden everyone went from wearing parallels or denims to wearing really silly clothes. It wasn't like that at all. It segued in slowly from the Sixties psychedelic era and went right through the punk thing and beyond really, because the early 1980s was another Glam boom. Also, nobody wore Glam stuff all the time. You would dress to suit the occasion.

'Black leather was very sexy and, whenever I wore it I got mistaken for Suzi Quatro, because we looked very similar. Again she is remembered as a Glam queen and all she ever wore was leather trousers and a leather jacket....and again, tight denims. I remember she was voted 'Rear of the Year' and, in that same daft contest, I came fourth. So she had a better bum than me.

'Noddy Holder was always, obviously, completely down to Earth. His version of Glam was the exact opposite of Bolan's. He never believed in this star thing. He wasn't precious. Far from it. He didn't believe his own press or anything like that. He was just Noddy and, for him, Glam meant wearing a daft hat and a silly suit. It didn't matter because Slade were just as really good rock band. Everyone knew that and the Glam thing was just an added extra. It was just something that groups did at the time. But for Marc it was the opposite. His Glam was more like glamour. The whole thing. It wasn't a joke to Marc. That was how he really was. But Slade were funny, like cartoons. See, I have a picture of Noddy on *Tiswas* and he's wearing a Freedom For Tooting T-shirt. That was his idea of Glam. Oh yes, and platforms. Slade wore platforms more than anyone. They were the platform kings.

'Sparks were fun, too. People warned us about them. Said that they took themselves too seriously. But they didn't. I think that some people didn't treat it as an act. And it was an act, with Ron Mael and the eyes. It was great, the kids in the studio would be transfixed by those eyes. I think that, today, they'd just regard him as a complete prat, or nerd or something.

'One of the television Glam fashions at the time would be the satin tour jackets. Record companies don't do this kind of thing anymore, but we were flooded with promotional items. We'd get dozens of tour jackets to hand out and to own the tour jacket of your favourite band was really *de rigeur* for a while. They'd be very garish sometimes, bright green, scarlet. You wouldn't, you just wouldn't wear one nowadays. It would be seen as the ultimate in naffness. I mean, you still get tour jackets but they now tend to have the band's name or album written in vary small lettering about the breast pocket or somewhere. It's very reserved now, very tasteful. Whereas, back then, there would be huge letters on the back saying SWEET TOUR or something. And if you had one you felt like you were in the business, like you were a bit special. There was that kind of naiveté that has gone.'

Ronald Dunkley directs films . . .

HORNES where 2 years credit comes easier than you thi

Left: the director's jacket. Not to be confused with a nice jacket. Above: Diana Rigg, relaxing with her glass-top coffee-table

Very Diana Rigg, very Sanderson.

Pa Pa Pa Pa Pa, Papapa,

The Glam era was immensely filmic in the scope of its vision, and the breadth of its collars. There were films which influenced Glam and there were films which reflected its impact on the world. There were Glam musicals, Glam sex flicks and Glam horror pics. The one unmissable (but unseeable in the UK) Glam film which managed to combine all the above aspects was Stanley Kubrick's *A Clockwork Orange*. On its release in 1971 there were legions of baggy-trousered teens queuing at Odeons around the country for a chance to view this stunning adaptation of Anthony Burgess' *book*. The film was a post-skinhead orgy of ultra-violence and sex, set bizarrely to a classical score. The leading role, Beethoven-loving teen thug Alex, was played by Malcolm McDowell, the criminally under-celebrated king of Glam film. McDowell's Alex was a cruel sardonic enigma that immediately affected British street fashion. (Even, at one point, causing skinhead gangs to wear comic false noses as disguises when engaging in 'unlawful activity'). *Clockwork Orange*'s bizarre soundtrack album, featuring a good deal of synthesised Beethoven, even took its place alongside Alice Cooper's *Killer* and David Bowie's *Rise And Fall Of Ziggy Stardust* in the record racks for a while. McDowell earned himself a significant cult following, as *Clockwork Orange* fans flocked to his later release *O Lucky Man* (1973) – which was a sequel to Lindsay Anderson's satirical proto-Glam *If* (1968).

Pa Pa Pa Pa Pa, Pa Pa Pa, Papapa, POW!

from WARNER BROS., A Warner Communications Company

This copyright advertising material is licensed and not sold and is the property of National Screen Service Ltd. and upon completion of the exhibition for which it has been licensed it should be returned to National Screen Service Ltd.

STANLEY KUBRICK'S CLOCKWORK ORANGE X   Starring MALCOLM McDOWELL · PATRICK MAG
ADRIENNE CORRI & MIRIAM KARLIN

Let's Do The Time Warp Again

'Ah, The Timewarp. A wonderfully tacky dance step from Richard O'Brien's *Rocky Horror Picture Show*, the travelling horror musical which managed to combine sex, horror and retro-rock 'n' roll Glam stomp all in one. It was made into a film in 1975 after selling out at theatres across Britain for two years. The film soon attracted a rabid following who copied the kitsch transvestite dress, sub-Alice Cooper eye make-up and sneer for middle-class, suburban priggishness as embodied by Brad and Janet. Audiences learned the dialogue by heart and shouted replies to questions at the screen, threw rice, water and flour over themselves in time to screen action, and performed the Timewarp in step with stars Tim Curry, Susan Sarandon, Richard O'Brien, Meatloaf and Christopher Biggins. Originally designed as a tribute to the RKO musicals of the 1930s, O'Brien's love of 1950s rock 'n' roll music and the camp over-dressing of the cast, combined with the sexually liberated theme (Tim Curry, the sweet transvestite from Trannsylvannia, singing to his beautiful male creation, "In just seven days, I can make you a ma-a-a-annnn!") to perfectly reflect the spirit of Glam.

Rock 'n' roll and sex (although no cross-dressing) figured heavily in two other defining Glam musicals. David Essex, always more content in the role of actor rather than pop star, managed to combine both occupations in *That'll Be The Day* and *Stardust*. Two films which saw his character rise from girl-hopping delinquency on a fairground to castle-owning pop stardom. The first release, chiefly filmed in Manchester's Belle Vue fairground sprawl, was the more evocative and powerful, reflecting, as it did, the retro fascination with rock 'n' roll (as evidenced by Essex's biggest hit single, Rock On).

By 1973 Glam music had grown big enough for its stars to warrant a film of their own. Marc Bolan, being the King of the Glam scene, made his own tour movie, *Born To Boogie*.

Surprisingly, it came and went quite swiftly, despite the presence of former Beatle Ringo Starr (who also took the cover photographs of Bolan for T.Rex's *Slider* LP in 1973), but Slade's semi-autobiographical *Slade In Flame* fared slightly better, and could still occasionally be seen at late night Saturday shows in assorted fleapits dotted around the UK coast as late as 1982.

The undisputed champion of Glam musical directors was Britain's own Ken Russell. It didn't matter that, The Who's rock opera *Tommy* apart, all of Ken's musicals used a symphonic score; they were all brash, bold and almost beautiful Glam extravaganzas. *Tommy* was the first example to attract Glam fans. The lavish direction and wild sets simply exude polish. Russell's tendency to impose grandiose treatment on a simple and often meaningless storyline all combine in a meticulously crafted and sculptured tackiness. Ken brilliantly buffed-up daftness rather than simply wallowing in it. His biopics of Mahler, Tchaikovsky (*The Music Lovers*) and Franz Liszt (the quite remarkable *Liszotmania*, complete with cannons as phalluses, fireworks and Roger Daltrey as lead) were Glam writ large and preposterous.

The American film industry had its own version of Glam which they referred to as Blaxploitation movies. Undoubtedly the best, and weirdest, hybrid Glam gangster/musicals came in the giant form of Richard Roundtree's slick *Shaft* trilogy. They had everything – great music from the likes of Isaac Hayes and Curtis Mayfield, social message, car chases, wild clothes and cool chicks in hot-pants. No wonder Quentin Tarantino would, twenty-five years later, raid the genre for actors and inspiration for his own *Jackie Brown*.

Fittingly perhaps, it was an American film which finally brought down the large red velvet curtain on the dominance of British Glam. John Travolta's gyrations in *Saturday Night Fever* were, like much else in Glam, cruelly underrated at the time of release, but in retrospect is now seen to have ushered in a new age – that of American Disco Glam. ☆☆

It Was The

Rising above lesser Glam horror flicks, *The Exorcist* spewed projectile vomit over the competition

Monster Mash

For some bizarre reason, as the Seventies dawned, people decide that they wanted to be frightened. Seriously frightened. So much so, that they would pay good money to sit together in darkened rooms and watch films that threatened to scare the living daylights out of them.

Hammer were still making their cardboard-set Victorian bodice-rippers and attempted, with *Hands of The Ripper* (1971), to introduce more gore into the proceedings in order to shock the platforms off their audience. It did manage to provoke some gasps alongside the laughs.

However, the most powerful cinematic experience of the Glam age was provided by *The Exorcist* (1973). A large scale, complex film that arrived surrounded by such an intimidating degree of hype that people, upon entering the cinema, genuinely believed that their lives would never be quite the same again. *The Exorcist* was a curiously beautiful film which had nothing in common with the endless stream of slash horror mutilation flicks which floundered in its wake but was, nonetheless, cheapened by their effect. It heralded a new era of large-budget horror movies.

Steven Speilberg, who'd made his name with a juggernaut horror film-for-TV, *Duel* (starring Dennis Weaver, then a big TV star for his title role of Cowboy detective *McCloud*) in 1971, made a big splash in cinemas with *Jaws* in 1975. Which was the same year that David Cronenberg first terrified film goers with his creepy, surreal *Shivers* (also known as *They Came From Within*), in which a slimy thing crawled out of the toilet and took over humans via sexual contact, leading to a brutal and bloody death. Nice. A year later both *Carrie* and *The Omen* would be unleashed into cinemas around the world. It all scared the life, literally, out of Glam. ☆☆

Ooooh, You

As a new decade began, the Swinging Sixties became the Swapping Seventies. Well, that is if you believe everything you see on the big screen. Britain's film industry in the early 1970s consisted of the odd James Bond film (too Sixties to be Glam) and two series of witless though gloriously politically incorrect films which used the double entendre as often as Slade used the major A chord. The *Confessions Of...* films, starring cute, wide-eyed urchin Robin Asquith, were as tacky as Blackpool on Bank Holiday Monday and managed to slip in more gratuitous innuendo than might be found in Sid James' wildest dreams. The hugely successful paperback novels and *Confessions* films managed to make the British suburbs seem as if all those net curtains were hiding a multitude of sinful activities.

Then there were the *Carry On* films. Sid, Hattie, Kenneth, Charles, Barbara and co. could, and did, wreak havoc with the English language and history – witness the theme to *Carry On Henry VIII* (1972), the chorus of which ends "…when good King Henry got his Hampton Court". In *Carry On Camping* (1972) Sid James got to wear Glam clothes and ogle Barbara Windsor's hot-pant clad bottom. Actually, that seemed to be the plot of all subsequent *Carry On* films, with only the scenery changing.

It was as if the world had decided that the sexual revolution had been successful, and soft porn was not only acceptable – it was de rigeur. Mary Millington became an

Above: Suddenly the NHS was seen in a whole new light. Right: The Carry On crew get ready for the first bus to Double Entendre

Are Awful!

overnight star by inviting people to *Come Play With Me*, taking her nurse uniform off and faking orgasm. Which she would continue to do in a string of badly-written excuses for lots of female nudity and wide-lapel suits until her sad, lonely demise. Imported American sex films were strictly hard core, and Linda Lovelace, the star of *Deep Throat*, became a household name despite nobody in Britain having seen the film (video still being a few years away). Glam sex films were as tacky as the

bands who'd strut their stuff on *Top Of The Pops*. They were laughably coy and incredibly naive. The soft porn film industry had been negligible until the Brits decided that they'd like to see simulated orgasm and positions that varied from the missionary. After *Emmanuel* in 1973, the industry tripled in turnover (forgive the pun). After *Emmanuel XXVIII* in 1980, the industry became strictly hard-core. And there's definitely no Glam in that.

Above: Robin Asquith gets to grips with Linda Bellingham in *Confessions Of A Driving Instructor*. Top right: *Carry On*'s Sid and Babs

Football, Beer and lots of Girls

George Best and the Roots of Glam with Mike Summerbee

The roots of Glam can be found in the mid-to-late Sixties, a pivotal period where post war austerity faded slowly, washed away by a wave of new prosperity. Encouraged by a media that had yet to grow cynical, freed into a brave new world of style, travel, music, sport, fashion, design and celebrity, Glam was brash, infectious and accessible. It might not have been the most aesthetically astute period in modern history, but it was fun. It was… Glam.

At the heart of this new colourful era, stood an unholy huddle of brash celebrities, based around the twin centres of swinging London (centred on the King's Road in Chelsea) and Manchester – a city dour no more, now the city of light. Manchester was at the time often referred to as 'the night-club capital of Europe' and blessed with two star-packed football teams, the celebrity-stacked Hollywood of the North (© Granada Television) danced to a constant backbeat of homegrown post-Merseybeat R 'n' B.

This was the new age of Glam and its vanguard were the celebrated George Best Set. Here we meet principal George Best-setter Mike Summerbee, the flying Manchester City and England winger who came into the city, wide-eyed and innocent, from rural Wiltshire. He soon found himself hurtling into the wild times of curiously innocent hedonism. With George Best – his mate, his business partner, his best man – by his side, Summerbee staggered from bar to bar, from match to match, from night club to night club and, until his wife Tina eventually intervened, from girl to girl.

Mike Summerbee says now, 'Manchester was amazing back then. You could

Mike Summerbee shortly after his fry-up

drive your car into the city centre, any kind of car, big flash car if you liked, park it easily, not bother locking it and just set off to the clubs. Me and Bestie would have a regular routine. We'd start off at the posh places and finish up, nine hours later, in the doss houses. We'd gradually drink our way downmarket, I think we must have become less discerning as the night wore on. Amazing clubs. We were treated like royalty. The Cabaret Club in Piccadilly, Mr Smith's – with DLT as resident DJ – Dino's, The Press Club, the Garden Of Eden. You want Glam? The Garden Of Eden had it all. Beautiful girls everywhere and they'd have tanks by the dance floor with crocodiles and alligators in them. Real flash stuff, that was. Then we'd go to Moss Side, to The Nile Club and loads of illicit drinking houses. It wasn't flash at all, we'd stumble out into the gutter. We got away with murder in those days…murder.

'We did a regular monthly series in the *Daily Express* called The George Best Set. That's where it came from. Me, Bestie and the girl known as Georgy Girl. She was Georgina Ellis, the daughter of Ruth Ellis. Really nice girl. We'd dress up in all kinds of things. Striped jackets, white trousers, straw boaters, all that kind of stuff, and we'd visit Chinese restaurants which were just becoming the places to go to. There would always be a photographer with us, snapping away, and those images of us living it up just seemed to define the times. People were suddenly doing things like going out for Chinese meals. It was almost as if we were leading them into a new lifestyle.

'Saturday nights were the best times. If George was playing away, I'd wait for the United coach to come back to Old Trafford and I'd pick him up and whisk him back to his landlady's house, in Chorlton-cum-Hardy. We'd have a quick tart up and then slide out into town. To the Roundtree's clubs; Roundtree's Sound and Roundtree's Spring Gardens. They were top places. Girls would suddenly appear on our arms. It was just like a dream. Everything laid on. Harry H. Corbett would come along. He was always in Manchester, Harry. He got a lot of his material from the characters we'd meet. We'd go to Fox's Revue Bar and would judge the stripping contest. The girls would try to entice us by wearing football rosettes on their G-strings. We'd pull them off – the rosettes – with our teeth. It was 1969. Manchester Stripper Of The Year Contest. They were all working girls and they would look after you if

'The thing then was lay-bys. It all happened in lay-bys. You pick a girl up, take her out for dinner or, in my case, Mackeson and a bag of crisps sometimes, and then you'd stop off in a lay-by on the way home. There'd be rocking cars with steamed up windows in lay-bys all over Manchester.'

you got into trouble, if you got too drunk and fell over. Not because you were a famous footballer. That's just how it was. Everyone was approachable. Anyone could go into Manchester on a Saturday night and wander up to me and George and have a chat. That illustrates just how much things have changed. This was the beginning of the big celebrity thing, and people were natural about it.

'The Grand Hotel in Manchester on Saturday mornings. All the press had their own bar and the players would go in and chat to them. We'd go in after the match, sometimes, too. Lots of players, drinking, chatting. Imagine that now. The reporters were real football reporters. They'd tell you what you had done wrong and you would listen. Many times the United lads would go in – Noel Cantwell, Denis Law, Denis Violet. And Malcolm Allison would pop in.

'We'd join up, have a meal with Matt Busby and Joe Mercer, then drift away to the clubs. A dozen clubs in one night, that was our boast. We were hard drinking, hard playing. Imagine players today, drinking until four in the morning on a regular basis. But we were so fit we could get away with it. It was an attitude of mind that we would take on the pitch. I don't think it ever affected our football. In fact, it had a positive side, because we were allowed to let ourselves really relax. Today's players, like my son Nicky, live in a different kind of glamour. It's really cynical now and totally false. If they are caught having half a lager at a bar someone will ring the club and report them. It's difficult for them to ever relax now because people will always have a pop at them. They are not even allowed to eat the things we ate. That might not be a bad thing. We had no set meals at all. Me and Bestie might be eating a full cooked breakfast in a Rusholme cafe at 10am before going to training. I remember going to play at Derby. We'd stop at the Mackford Arms on the way and have sausage, bacon, beans, fried bread, three rounds of toast, pot of tea, the full works, and then we'd relax, have a drink and, after that, go and play the match. Now it's just pasta for them. I'm always telling Nicky to have a steak. He looks as though he needs one.

'The most celebrity stacked place was the Film Exchange. Everyone was in there and everyone knew you. Laurence Olivier would be eating his dinner, you'd stand at the bar drinking with Dennis Waterman. Or drink rum and milk with Michael Elphick. Just lots and lots of drinks. Tarby would come in, Bill Roache, Richard Beckinsale, and the old Herman's Hermits would be around. It was overwhelming for me because it happened so fast, from local footballing notoriety in Swindon to being at the centre of this goldfish bowl in the most exciting city in the world. The photographers would always be hovering and we loved it because they would never take any really nasty shots. They certainly could have done. Me and Bestie rolling drunk in the gutter. Staggering into seriously dubious drinking dens, playing cards…and all kinds of women. Imagine the photos that could have been taken.

'The thing then was lay-bys. It all happened in lay-bys. You pick a girl up, take her out for dinner or, in my case, Mackeson and a bag of crisps sometimes, and then you'd stop off in a lay-by on the way home. There'd be rocking cars with steamed up windows in lay-bys all over Manchester. It's funny, because you'd walk out with a girl right under the eyes of a photographer and they never thought about following you. Imagine that now. Be on the front page of the *News Of The World* every week.

In The Summertime

Mike Summerbee on the Magaluf Experience

'**It was the time when people** first started to go on holidays abroad. Before that it had either been the Isle Of Man or, I suppose, Blackpool. But suddenly there were these exotic destinations in Spain. Bestie and me went and stayed six weeks in the Atlantic Hotel in Magaluf. It was a tremendously exotic thing to do and the papers were full of it. It was the only hotel in Magaluf and they were desperate to attract people from Britain. So me and George flew out with Iberia Airlines on their very first flight, the night flight. It felt like breaking new ground. As if the whole of Manchester would follow us. And so they did, in a way. It was VIP treatment, loads of drinks on the plane and photographs of us both relaxing, drinking, stretching out. That was the impression people must have got about flying, that you could stretch out and relax and a scantily-clad girl would keep topping up your champagne glass. It wasn't quite like that on the charter flights, was it? But we spent six weeks at that hotel. We actually ran out of money after four weeks, but it didn't matter because people kept coming up to us and buying us drinks. Phenomenal situation, and I know the papers reported on us back home, so it was good PR for the hotel and for Magaluf in general. We were on a bit of a winner, really!

'We were incredibly naïve. We went to Australia on a Comet. We thought it was just going round the corner but it was a 36-hour flight. After 22 hours it dawned on us just how far it was. We decided that perhaps we'd better stop drinking for a while.'

I've Got My Blue Jeans On...

Mike Summerbee (below) on footballers' 'style'

'This was the period when footballers suddenly became stylish – or not, depending how you view it. But me and Bestie were doing fashion shoots in all the papers and we had our boutique – Edwardia – up and running in Manchester. For me it was the beginning of a new career in shirt-making, which went from being really trendy to bespoke tailoring, which I still do today. Footballers in the past had just worn the same clothes as their supporters, so we also found ourselves spearheading all this fashion stuff, which was really weird. People paying you to wear certain clothes. There were other Glam footballers, of course. Peter Marinello, obviously, and it practically ruined him. Rodney Marsh, Peter Bonnetti, Alan Hudson, Frank Worthington… Suddenly they were all in really wild suits with big ties and jackets with huge collars.

'But I think I'm right in saying that Manchester City led the way on the field. They had a style that matched the flamboyant way they played. It might have been a reaction against United because they were always seen as the glamour club and we were the working class oiks. But the kit thing started to take off. I really loved the Man City sky-blue cotton shirts, and when they added the maroon and white tops to the socks that was seen as a really bold fashion statement. You'd see kids everywhere, not just in Manchester, but all over the country, in Manchester City kits. We definitely had the edge on United in terms of style then. And the big one, of course, came with the introduction of the black and red striped away kit with black shorts. Now, that really was cool. I think we swiped it off AC Milan and, in a sense, that made it even better. Suddenly there was Italian design on British football pitches. And those shirts spread like wildfire. They really were everywhere. United fans would even buy them. They also felt fantastic to wear at a match, really, to be wearing that kit meant feeling invincible. It's probably no accident that we won the FA Cup and the Cup Winners Cup wearing that red and black. After City other clubs starting taking their kits far more seriously.

'Today's shirts are not the same. They're 100 per cent polyester. No wonder they smell. These shirts were 100 per cent cotton. That's why you could see the sweat on the players. I hate those new shirts, cheap, nasty and ugly. A few years ago, at the testimonial for Matt Busby's 80th, me and Bestie were given some big old cotton shirts to wear. We put them on and looked at each other. George said, 'Hey, these aren't too bad…' We walked out thinking we were invincible again. Thinking we could play again. Of course, we couldn't.'

Belfast Boy

'Where's me shirt?' asks George Best

'**I've said it a few times,** but I blame the Seventies for the demise of the football strip into the artless mess it is today. The problems began in the Seventies and I suppose we played our part. When the Seventies began, I had my hair over my shoulder, my flares were ludicrous and the knots in my ties were simply massive. That was the style, and I cut a dash in the bars of Manchester with Mike and our friends, but I think, because of the position I was in I dressed a little more outrageously than the norm. Fashion was big and had no subtlety at all. Call it Glam if you will, it was just loud, everything loud. Big collars and bright colours. When the Seventies started, fashion and football were on different planets. Yeah, we had our boutique and some of the flasher players had picked up a bit of money from modelling. We all did those home delivery magazines, that kind of thing.

'But it hadn't affected football, not on the pitch. Football was very naïve at the start of the Seventies. It was only waking up to things like sponsorship and the kits we wore were still pretty plain. We didn't need colourful strips with flashes and designs all over them. The characters on the pitch were colourful enough. At first I thought the strip changes were a really good thing. There was Don Revie's England in '74, who started looking flash. And Derby County, I think, were the first team to press for shirt sponsorship. That was the thin end of the wedge. I look at football strips today with a certain amount of sadness… and maybe we were a little bit to blame. Just think back, though, to the time when a kid in the street could wear a white t-shirt and a pair of blue shorts and think he was wearing an England kit. That's not too long ago.'

'We had extreme times. But it was always totally one thing or another. The great thing about those days was that although we tasted this huge glamour thing, we were still living in the real world. So we'd live a life of absolute extremes. No in-betweens. I would go drinking with the lads down the pub one night and be a guest of the Prime Minister the next day.'

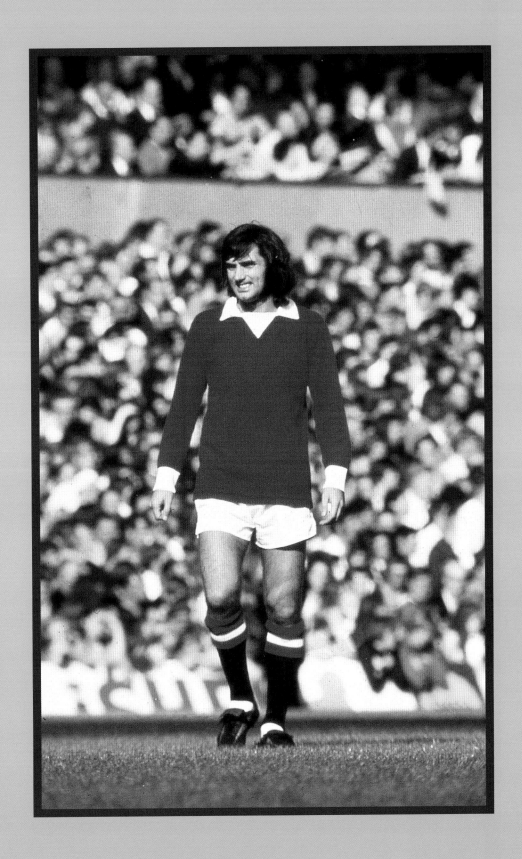

You're Going Home In A ****** Ambulance

George Best on Leeds United

'**That Leeds team are now remembered** as the most cynical football team of all time. Although they did deserve that reputation, I hated playing against them, I really did. It must be remembered that they also had a hell of a lot of skill, too, but they were still a bloody nightmare. But my little anecdote tends to sum them up. It concerns Matt Busby who, in a team talk before meeting Leeds, went through each member of their side. It must be remembered that Busby loved Man United but he was also a fiercely patriotic Scot.

'Anyway, Matt went like this: "Gary Sprake, the goalkeeper… on his day a nasty piece of work. Right back, Paul Reaney…dirty bastard. Left back, Terry Cooper…even dirtier bastard. Johnny Giles…dirty little bastard. Centre half, Jack Charlton…dirty big bastard. Left half, wee Billy Bremner… good Scottish boy!"
'

Those Were The Days

Mike Summerbee

'**There is this famous story about George...** After he had won one night at a casino and a bellboy found him in his hotel room drinking champagne with Miss World and twenty five grand scattered across his bed. The bell boy said, "Tell me George, where did it all go wrong?" Well, there are a few variations to that story but it really does sum up what life was like for a while. There was a period when the papers started writing a lot of bad stuff but, in some ways, it didn't seem too bad at all. We were having a fantastic time and yet some of the public would be sympathetic towards us. All that "It's terrible. You are ruining yourselves!" stuff. People would look really concerned and would tell us that we were heading towards ruin. And we'd be stood there, surrounded by mini-skirted girls drinking free champagne and trying not to talk about our day jobs, which were hardly difficult, were they? We were paid to play football. Now, how can anyone say we were in trouble at that point?

Of course it did turn sour, especially for George, but he had a hell of a lot of fun, especially in Manchester. That was the ultimate Glam experience, wasn't it? For today's famous footballers, and I meet a lot of them through my son, Nicky, it's horrible. The press don't look after you any more. They are not on your side anymore. They don't write about football. They always need an angle. Believe me, we had great times.'

Bestie with Parkie and three Dollies. Where'd it all go wrong, George?

The View From The Terrace

Post-match Terrences, Venables and Mancini, decide the only way to stay cool is to drink the bubbly naked

Meanwhile, down South, you'd have thought that the Sixties hadn't been too unkind to football. The decade had started with the Spurs double-winning team, the greatest side that there had ever been. England won the World Cup. Spurs won the FA Cup in 1967. On the surface, it looks OK, right? Well, yes and no. The Sixties had sown the seeds for a grim future. Winning the World Cup, while a Godsend in terms of attracting attention and popularity to the game, was a terrible thing. You're not really supposed to say things like that but, hey! We don't care.

Sir Alf Ramsey, Dagenham Alf, had created a team devoid of flair, bereft of style. Possessing the greatest goal-scorer of the modern era, he rejected Jimmy Greaves in favour of the more workman-like Geoff Hurst. Don't worry – we're not going to go into a huge treatise on the state of the modern game, it's just to say that, in winning, Sir Alf took the joy out of the game. If proof be needed, you've only got to look at how the Seventies began: with Arsenal winning the Double. Could anything be more depressing?

It was into this scenario that – yes – our Glam players emerged. They were players who flaunted their skill in the face of the footballing authorities. Dandies blessed with the sense not to tow the line, they created their own little world with its own little rules. Like all artists, they got away with it because they were outrageously talented. Rodney Marsh, Charlie George, Frank Worthington, Alan Husdon, Stan Bowles, Tony Currie... Loved by the fans and reviled by the Establishment, these players were the pop stars of their world. It wasn't only their talent that set them apart (though God knows, that was enough), it was their *joie de vivre*, the way they played the game. When someone like Marsh or Bowles got into their stride, taking the piss out of the hard grey men around them, they were saying to the fans, 'It doesn't have to be like that. You can be like me. You can be like me if you adopt my value system and don't buy into theirs.' No wonder they were seen as a threat. No wonder they won about two-and-a-half caps between them.

Each was ridiculously talented and, between them, they are responsible for the 1990s surge in interest in Seventies football. Kitsch hair, sideburns you could grow tomatoes in and talent to die for, they represent something now, something maverick that in the corporate Nineties touches a nerve.

Pick your own, but without question the most Glamtastic of the lot was Frank Worthington. Frank was an Elvis fan. Fan? Fan is short for fanatic and that's what Frank was. When we met, one of the first questions he asked was, 'Are you a fan of the King?' It seemed churlish to ask the king of where. Even now, he was wearing the clothes. An electric blue jacket, black shirt – natch – and black and white Fifties shoes. Pointy sideburns. 'People say I've squandered a fortune on birds and booze, but as my old mate Stan Bowles said, it's better than wasting it.' It's a gag the ancient Greeks used – and even then it was nicked. Frank lived his whole career in the footballing backwaters. Bolton, Huddersfield,

A stiff drink and several Woodbines – the only way for John Radford and Charlie George to follow 90 minutes of football

Leicester, places like that. Liverpool did put in a bid for him and the deal was almost done. All that was left to do was the final medical. It revealed high blood pressure. And why was your blood pressure high, Frank? 'It was what you might call living a little bit too much in the fast lane.'

What can I tell you about Frank? In 1967, a young player on the way up, he managed to secure tickets to the Spurs v Chelsea Cup Final. It was a dream, going to Wembley to see the FA Cup Final. Frank got to London, had a bit of a think and… 'I shouldn't really tell you, but I sold my ticket and headed off down the Kings Road.' Twelve years later, playing for Bolton against Ipswich, he scored the goal that everyone remembers. There's Frank, his back to the Ipswich goal, juggling the ball on his left foot. Looking around at who to pass to – that's a gag, by the way – he noticed that the Ipswich defence had followed him out. A smile. He flicked the ball over his shoulder, spun around, ran past the astonished defenders and volleyed the ball into the net. Audacious, outrageous, perfect.

Sometimes winning a game came a poor second to the size of the quote marks...

It wasn't just the players. For managers, the choice was both more and less stark. They wouldn't go down the peacock route – being that much older than the players, it was that much harder for them. But they could do something that the players could never do. Unlike them, managers were individuals. They didn't have to fit into a mould, they didn't have to work in a unit. They were also higher up the food chain than players. They could take the piss in a way that players couldn't because they had more authority. In a similar relationship they were, in turn, subject to the whims of their chairmen, but that's another story. Managers had to inspire people, but they were the lion-tamers, not the lions. They could project any image they wanted. Theirs was not a team game.

So they went down a different route, something that combined traditional male values with traditional (working) class desires: money. The signifiers were bought with cash (on a first names basis).

Natural showmen, they took to their task like elephants to castles. But they were more than showmen. They were more than team players. Riding high on the burgeoning cult of the individual, they were determined to do things their way. Though they'd deny it, it sometimes seemed as if the winning came a poor second to the size of the quote marks. The figures that counted were the column inches, not the 'points for' total, and the notion of being publicly quoted had very little to do with the stock market.

Things really changed during the 1970 World Cup. Even though England had its best ever team there, it was nothing to do with the football. It was during that World Cup that the panel was born. Ostensibly a group of talking head experts brought in to offer analysis, what the panel actually did was create a platform for show-offs. And show off they did. It's no coincidence that the first batch included Malcolm Allison, Brian Clough and Jack Charlton. Mouths vied with mouths as these 'personalities' fought to get the biggest laugh or, more often, to say the most outrageous thing. Everyone knew that the more outrageous the comment, the bigger tomorrow's headline would be.

Jason King takes to the pitch. No, my mistake, it's Frank Worthington

And if you were going to sound outrageous, then you had to look outrageous too. For pop's glitter and sparkle, read shades and leather. Over everything was the quintessential sheepskin coat. There was the all-weather suntan. (Let's not forget that back then a suntan was desirable because it showed that you were wealthy enough to be able to afford a holiday in the sun.) The gold identity bracelet. Blow-dried hair. The shoes – Gucci – were leather slip-ons, the type with the little gold chain across the top. The tie was one of those dual purpose efforts: it acted as an effective scarecrow and, if the weather turned, you could happily camp out in it. As the right-hand was holding a glass of Moët, the left furiously puffed at a Havana, while the mouth spat out an endless patter of quotable quips. One-liners that sounded as if they couldn't make up their minds whether they wanted to be Bill Shankly or Jimmy Tarbuck.

It was a curious time for football, caught between the economic austerity of the Sixties and the current money era. It was a time that allowed for the individual – characters as they were euphemistically called. It was a window in time. You know the funny thing about it? Everyone knocked Big Frank, saying how he was a dilettante – OK, they probably said 'poof' but you know what we mean – how he wasn't committed, how his blood pressure was high. But Frank played on until he was 49.

Because he could. I like that.

I'm Just A Jeepster For Your Love

When rock 'n' roll was born the songs were about two things: sex and cars. At the time one was not possible without the other. In the America of the mid-1950s teenagers had to drive, not only so that they could play chicken in 1940s Ford coupes at the edge of California cliffs, but so that they could produce a baby-boom of their own from the back seat of Dad's old Edsel.

In Britain, rock 'n' roll was about the same things, but car ownership took a little longer to reach the same proportions as they had in the States. Some British car manufacturers had enjoyed a pretty good time in the 1960s. Jaguar had crossed the cultural and class divide with both white collar saloons (the Mk II) and the E-Type sports car (which was cheaper than a packet of wine gums at the time), while Triumph had put out the very fast Herald Vitesse and GT6 at almost affordable prices. But you wouldn't see very many examples of these cars outside the leafy suburbs. By 1970 Britain's inner cities still reverberated predominantly to the sound of Ford, Austin and Vauxhall exhausts. Some of which might have looked almost Glam – the Cortina 1600E and the Mini for instance – but the majority of which were boxy, rust-prone and utilitarian. No one could ever pretend that the Austin 1100, Vauxhall Viva or Ford Anglia were Glam. There were still, at this time, precious few Japanese cars in the UK, and only slightly more Italian, French

and German models – although of course the VW Beetle and Beetle van had been imported by numerous Australasian hippies, their sills stuffed with hashish – and Scandinavian motors still powered more jets than cars. Things had to change. The country was getting bored with boxes on wheels. Men's lapels and trousers were getting wider, women's heels were getting higher and schoolkids were too embarrassed to be seen in their parent's Ford Prefect. The rock 'n' roll kids of the Fifties were grown up and wanted their own car in which to show off, drive fast and still carry the family around.

Enter the Ford Capri.

Ever since Steve McQueen had bounced over San Francisco hills in a Ford Mustang fastback in *Bullitt* (1968), the design staff at Ford's Dagenham headquarters had been desperate for a version for themselves. Rumour has it that they'd all been wearing black polo neck jumpers to work, too. The Mustang was too big for the UK's tiny trunk roads. The Capri, however, was perfect. It had the lines and, if you squinted hard enough, the pedigree of the Mustang. Unfortunately, originally it only had the 1300 and 1600 engine from the Cortina under its long, shapely bonnet when first launched in 1969. As everything got Glam in 1970 though, the Dagenham boys got around to wedging the Essex straight-six from a Zodiac under the lid, and Hey Presto! The first Glam motor was born. Ford dared to compare the car with the BMW 3.0 CS Coupe, the Mercedes Benz 350 SL Coupe and the Aston Martin DBS V8 It was slower (top speed 122mph, 0-60 in 11.4 seconds) but it was a hell of a lot cheaper – £1,321 against the BMW's £3,118, Merc's £5,601 and Aston's £8,349.

The Capri proved so successful, mainly due to the fact that the bulging bonnet of the 3.0 litre was kept for the 1300 and 1600 versions, that Ford revamped the Cortina, playing on its rallying success to sell the MkIII which came in suitably Glam colours – yellow, orange, silver, brown (with black vinyl roof), purple and red. The new model was fat and flared and bore a passing resemblance to the American muscle cars revving out of Detroit at the time. Neither the Capri nor the Mk III Cortina would outlast the

Glam era, with the former adopting a more business-like look (plus 2.0 and 2.8 litre engines) and TV fame as the car of choice for Bodie and Doyle in *Sweeney*-rip off *The Professionals* in 1977, and the latter getting boxy again for the rust-prone Mk IV in 1977, which was very unloved by everyone, including mini-cab drivers (and they find it hard to dislike any car). As well as the Cortina getting the flared treatment, its little brother the Escort had a make-over in 1970 when the Mexico model (the World Cup was played in Mexico that year) was introduced, bearing bright paint, flared arches and sporty alloy wheels. It proved to be the only classic non-specialist Escort.

Top: Glam fashion and motion in perfect harmony – the Levi's Mini. Nice. Above: The Austin Princess, a wedge on wheels. Top right: The Ford Mustang, Glam US-style. Below: the Ford Escort Mexico, Gordon Banks should have saved his

Not to be outdone, Austin decided that they would produce a Glam car for discerning middle class suburban swingers using a name which had earned prestige in the 1960s when the company had used a Rolls Royce engine for a limited edition Princess Vanden Plas. The Glam version of the Princess had a radical wedge-shaped body, the bonnet of which raked so low that drivers were forever banging the nose of the car into bollards, low walls and small children. The engine was an Austin 2.2 litre unit which used more petrol per mile than an oil tanker, and the body was made of raw, untreated pig iron which would turn to rust and cause whole panels to casually fall off in the slightest Spring shower.

Meanwhile, down the A40 in Oxford, Morris were busy tuning their previously pedestrian Marina, and dipping the bodies in deep purple, electric blue and bright yellow paint. The Marina twin-carb turned a dull 1800 engine into a sporty, racy, throbbing unit which, when the steering wheel was trimmed in leather, meant that the driver became Mario Andretti. Or James Hunt. Anyway, it was enough to persuade the makers of *The Sweeney* that George Carter could drive one and get tyre squeals out of it in a chase with a Vauxhall Victor (a very un-Glam car, despite having flared wheel arches and a column-gear change).

The Sweeney was *the* programme for bestowing Glam status on a car. Which is why the Ford

Right: the Ford Transit – in this colour combo, the Gary Glitter of the automobile world

Transit, Granada (which used the same 3.0 litre engine as the Capri), and especially its fastback brother, the Consul GT, were U-Glam. Vinyl roof (or factory-fitted peel-back sunroof), an eight-track cartridge stereo, black and chrome sports wheels, warm leatherette seats and a side view which, at 100 paces, could pass for an American motor, the Granada had it all. Plus, most importantly, it was less than the price of a semi-detached suburban home.

The Capri, Marina, Cortina, Granada and Princess were family cars which doubled as a sports car for those *Jason King* and *Persuaders* fans who had no chance of ever getting a truly Glam car like a Jensen Interceptor, Ferrari Dino, Aston Martin DBS or even Triumph Stag (sold with the snappy slogan 'Keeping up with the Triumph Stag is no problem if you've got the money'). These were everyday cars which, with a little bit of imagination, could be turned into exotic Glam wagons. And they were.

Jeremy Clarkson's Top Five Glam Motors:

1. Ford Capri 3.0 Ghia
2. Morris Marina Twin Carb
3. Ford Granada Consul fastback
4. Ford Escort Mexico
5. Triumph Stag

Manchester City and England footballer Mike Summerbee:

'Cars were a big thing for us players. George (Best) had loads of sports cars – his Lotus Europa was great. I had fantastic cars. One of them was the P1800 Volvo. A Simon Templar car, complete with red upholstery. It had a record player in it which would play 45s. Somehow the record would never jump, even when you went over bumps. That was a really cool motor, driving through Cheshire in the summer, playing Working In A Coalmine or The In Crowd, lots of Motown, stuff like that. Of course, I also had an E-Type Jag. Long nose. It was almost obligatory for footballers to have E-Types...sexiest car of all time. But my favourite car was a dark blue Daimler automatic. Very Glam. I saw it in a car lot in Stretford when I was on my way to play with England in America. I bought it on the way back and immediately used it to drive down to my mother's house in Devon.'

ABC, easy as...

A is for A-Line skirts, the replacement for the mini, which thankfully covered flared-thighs, and in their Maxi incarnation allowed a soft landing on falling from ridiculous platform shoes.

B is for Bolan. Marc, the elfin prince of Glam. He'd tried Mod, he'd tried Hippie, but he was Born To Boogie. R.I.P.

C is for Cresta. The coolest ad campaign of the Seventies. The Bear that inspired The Fonz (no, really). The drink that stripped paint.

D is for Dougal in *Magic Roundabout*. A former toilet brush turned-TV star who was so laid-back he would fall asleep during the programme. Hippies preferred Dylan the rabbit, man, which is why they never managed to change the world.

E is for Excess. More was very definitely more in Glam – more hair, more height, more glitter, more guitars, more drugs, more More (long, thin, black cigarettes favoured by Telly Savalas in *Kojak*). Moderation had ceased to exist.

Wham Bam Thank You GLAM!

F is for Fray Bentos. 'Steak pie'-in-a-tin. Had a wonderful catchline in the TV ad: "It's Beef! It's Beef!" These days you wouldn't feed it to your dog, but it was *so* Glam because it was Steak. Serve with Blue Nun and Smash.

G is for G-Spot, much discussed by feminists, much misunderstood by Glam males who thought it was a bit of the A40 where you could drive very fast ('pulling Gs') in their MG Austin 1300, without crashing.

H is for Hunt the Shunt. Britain's coolest Grand Prix driver. James Hunt (left) smoked fags while he was racing! He wore too much gold jewellery! He crashed – a lot! He could drink Oliver Reed under the table! He got all the best birds! He won the F1 World Championship without sleep!

I is for Interior Design. Until Glam it was simply a D.I.Y. pursuit. After, it was a lifestyle statement. The colours were Puce, Red, Yellow, Blue, Green, Purple and Brown. There were swirls everywhere; on the ceilings, on the walls, on the floors and even on the windows. The furniture was as bright as the walls, and the overhead lights had to be able to be pulled down on a curly lead. (see *Wallpaper** magazine).

J is for John Player Specials. The Glammest of Glam fags, they came in a black box with gold lettering. They were the sponsors of the British F1 race-winning Lotus team. Lotus were so grateful for the funding that they designed a car which looked like the JPS packet, and did it out in JPS colours (the Europa).

K is for Key Parties. 'Swingers' would throw their car keys into a pot in the middle of a swirly-pattern carpeted room, have a few Campari and sodas and then pick out a set of car keys from the pot. Men with helmet-hair would inevitably end up with their mate's wife who they'd always hated, fail to get it up and end up shaving off that Zapatta moustache. The only scenario worse than this was if a macho man ended up with his own wife and enjoyed it.

L is for Loon Pants, the flares which hippies would wear without thinking that they were Glam Kids. They could only be bought by post from a company that advertised in the back of the *NME*, and had to be worn with a Led Zep t-shirt and Jesus boots. A very big factor in the birth of Punk – anyone seen wearing a pair after January 1 1976 got a good kicking.

M is for Metallic (and medallion). If it moved, it had to be sprayed with metallic paint. Cars, shoes, hair, shirts, guitars, Y-fronts and faces. To be truly Glam, it had to be Spangly, and preferably hung around the neck, nestling among a thatch of chest hair thick enough to lose small animals in. Although it would truly come of age during Disco, the medallion made a few prominent appearances during Glam (see Oliver Tobias).

N is for Helmut Newton, a 'fashion' photographer who managed to persuade high class models to get their kit off for a series of 'artistic poses' which would challenge the middle classes' perception of the eroticism of art. Actually it was just soft porn.

O is for Oliver Tobias. At the height of Disco fever, Tobias played the lead role in Joan Collins' finest hour and a half, *The Stud*, but during Glam's heyday he was Britain's answer to Warren Beatty – all tight shirts, hipster jeans, cleft chin, feather-cut bouffant and a permanent smirk which said "I've just had a shag". In the late 1960s, he had been the lead in the British version of Hair, something he was not short of, thus guaranteeing a career in Glam.

P is for *Please Sir*. Ultimately Glam was all about school. Just as rock 'n' roll was in the beginning, Glam was about the power of the teenager to influence all aspects of life. Which is why *Please Sir* was the Glammest of all sit-coms. English teacher John Alderton was deadly dull and anti-Glam, but his class, a kind of Bash Street Kids gone to Pot, were undeniably Glam: Duffy was a denim-clad football hooligan who must have been at least five years older than Alderton but sported a great Rod Stewart hair cut; Sharon was a mini-skirted, skinny-rib jumpered, feather-cut dolly bird; and even Maureen, the skinny, mousy girl with a crush on Sir, wore Glam gear.

Q is for Queers. With everyone from Malcolm MacDonald to the brickie your sister was going out with indulging in a spot of cross-dressing, with pop stars flinging open their closets to reveal the skeleton of a Gay life, being 'queer' was no longer such a deadly disease. It still didn't do to flaunt it too much, but at least being able to hold hands with someone that Granny wasn't sure was a boy or a girl was possible without getting duffed up.

R is for Richard Allen, author of all those *Skinhead* and *Suedehead* books who took on Glam and, as ever, got it right royally wrong – especially in *Teenybopper Idol*: "Bobby Sharp is the newest star in a growth of youthful worship… But showbusiness expertise and talent are not enough – a star like Bobby needs a manager who doesn't know the meaning of ethics and when it comes to exploitation the Teeny Boppers are a gift of the kind he knows how to manipulate." Huh?

S is for Sweets: Spangles – nothing on earth (and probably in space) tasted as weird; Curly Wurly – a soft, chewy crochet of toffee and chocolate which was advertised by a forty-year old man (Terry Scott) dressed as a schoolboy; Lovehearts – sold as being fizzy sweets (tasted like three-day old Dr Pepper) which had cute love messages on them. Girls would send them to David Cassidy and Donny Osmond addressed simply, 'America'; Bounty – coconut and chocolate bars that offered 'a taste of paradise' and a crafty butchers at scantily-clad birds; Cadbury's Flake – marked the invention of fellatio; and Turkish Delight – a grown-ups' chocolate bar that hinted at naughty exoticism. The ad campaign used sheiks, sand, snakes and veiled women doing belly dances.

T is for Twister, a children's game appropriated by parents to get their parties off to a swinging start. Also worth a mention: Kerplunk!, Buckaroo, Mousetrap and a host of other games which used as many plastic bits as possible, thus ensuring they were unplayable after three days because something would invariably go missing.

U is for Unions. They ruled the country and made things great. Even Donkey Jackets were Glam. Who wouldn't want a three-day working week, national minimum wage, safe working conditions, and bargaining power over capitalist swine growing fat on the blood, sweat and tears of the working man? Apparently nobody, which is why the Great British public voted in Margaret Thatcher at the first opportunity.

V is for Valium. Originally introduced to calm down all those sex-crazed suburban housewives, the downer was soon appropriated by Glam Kids who loved to mix it with other drugs: barbiturates, speed, booze, you name it. Is it any wonder that the students stopped revolting?

W is for Women's Lib. For the first time, men got to see women's underwear in daylight.

X is for Xanadu. The name chosen for every dodgy disco with a coke-sniffing owner who thought he was Warren Beatty but bore more resemblance to Warren Mitchell.

Y is for Yucca. For the first time, plants made their way into the house. Glam homes had to have a Yucca or two in the dining room. Their pots would inevitably be filled with JPS butts and cheap cigarillos after Saturday night dinner parties at which the guests would don velvet dinner suits and backless evening gowns, listen to Bert Kaempfert records and eat fondue.

Z is for Zebedee from *Magic Roundabout*. He'd always come along and ruin things by sending us all to bed while he got to stay up and take drugs with Dylan, the rabbit. Is it any coincidence that he looked like Frank Zappa?

No More Heroes

After five glorious Glam years, the world changed for ever. A different style of dressing up caught on, a new movement was born – the boy looked at Johnny, and liked what he saw. Clothes were ripped, make-up was plastered on eyes with a trowel, cheeks were pierced with safety-pins, nobody smiled. The simple pleasures of glitter and gloss were all too quickly forgotten.

Flares and big hair stayed in fashion for a while, enjoying a wild time in discos around the world until well into the 1980s, but the Glam bands of Britain woke up one morning in February 1976 and found that they had been confined to endless nostalgia tours around seaside piers, holiday camps and bingo halls. Many of them are still doing the scampi-in-a-basket circuit, enjoying the beer and laughs, even if the new band members get younger than the audience by the week.

Of course Glam didn't change the world. It just felt as though it did for all those starry-eyed boys and girls who wrecked their foot arches on gigantic heels, and are now worrying about their own daughters doing the same in those daft-looking platform trainers. Ultimately, it was a good laugh. Don't let anyone tell you differently.

Call it the Spaceball Ricochet. ☆☆

Photographs

Advertising Archives	pages 136, 137, 140, 141, 143
British Motor Industry Heritage Trust	pages 136, 138
Bravo	page 92
Coloursport	pages 123, 129, 131, 132, 133, 135
Corbis	pages 14, 15
Ford	pages 136, 137, 138, 139
Ronald Grant Archive	pages 88, 90, 115, 118, 120
Sally James personal collection	pages 67, 96, 97, 98, 110
Pictorial Press	pages 9, 12, 16, 23, 27, 28, 29, 31, 32/33, 41, 47, 49, 50, 53, 55, 61, 63, 65, 68, 87, 93, 94, 99, 100, 102, 105, 07, 120, 121, 137, 138, 141
Rex	page 140
SIN	pages 75, 76
Mike Summerbee personal collection	page 127
Vintage Magazine Company	pages 8, 10, 113

This was a JMP Ltd production – special thanks to David Knight for the super silver platform shoes, Jessica Dodds for her photographs of them and all the other Glam paraphenalia (which she is too young to remember) and Joshua Sims for making with the witty captions (how old are you?). A big thank you to all those who shared their memories of the Glam years with us – Sally James, Pan's People, Mike Summerbee, George Best, David Enthoven, Noddy Holder, Les Gray, Frank Worthington and, in memoriam, Brian Connolly. Bless.

P.S. The views of the authors expressed in this book are not necessarily those of JMP Ltd. We think that Alice Cooper and the Bay City Rollers were Glam.